Ask Ed

Marijuana Gold—

Trash to Stash

by Ed Rosenthal
with S. Newhart

QUICK AMERICAN ARCHIVES

Ask Ed: Marijuana Gold—Trash to Stash
Copyright ©2002 Quick Trading Company

Published by Quick American Archives
A division of Quick Trading Company
Oakland, California
www.quicktrading.com

ISBN 13: 978-0-932551-52-8
EBOOK ISBN: 978-1-936807-0-24

Project Management: S. Newhart
Product Research: Jaloola
Cover Design: Timothy Horn Design
Interior Design, Typesetting and Illustration: Lightbourne

We wish to thank all the individuals and companies who provided information and products for review.

Publisher's Cataloging-in-Publication
(Provided by Quality Books, Inc.)

Rosenthal, Ed.
    Ask Ed : marijuana gold : trash to stash / Ed
Rosenthal. -- 1st ed.
    p. cm.
    Includes bibliographical references.
    ISBN 0-932551-52-1

    1. Marijuana--Processing. 2. Cannabis--Composition.
I. Title.

HV5822.M3R67 2002   362.295
                               QBI33-644

The material offered in this book is presented as information that should be available to the public. The Publisher does not advocate breaking the law. However, we urge readers to support the secure passage of fair marijuana legislation.

Did he doubt or did he try?
Answers aplenty in the bye and bye.
Talk about your plenty, talk about your ills,
One man gathers what another man spills.

from *St. Stephen*
© Garcia, Lesh, Hunter
Courtesy Grateful Dead

CONTENTS

INTRODUCTION

THE idea for a "Trash to Stash" book has been sifting through my mind for many years. It all started around 1987 with the late John Gallardi and his "Master Sifter." His unit used vibrations to knock the glands from grass. It was the first commercial unit available for the purpose. He also made a rolling tray/sifter with a stainless steel mesh surface and a sliding glass gland collector.

About the same time that John was working on his trays, Nevil Schumacher of the Seed Bank showed me a piece of "water hash" he had made with Rob Clarke. It was an amazingly hard ball. Nevil chipped a piece off of the brittle material. When he lit it in a pipe, it melted and bubbled. Then he told me they had made the amazingly potent ball from leaf and trim.

Years before, in 1979, the "Tilt Pipe" a sophisticated globe-type vaporizer was marketed. Unfortunately, the venture was doomed to failure because the War on Drugs was starting its upward trajectory. Paraphernalia was outlawed, and since the Tilt had no other use than vaporizing pot, it became illegal, with no redeeming tobacco value. With this device, you could use the low-quality pot generally available at the time and just inhale the essence. It made quite a difference.

I was intrigued with developing uses for leaf and trim, known in many grower circles as trash. My reasoning was simple. These "waste" products usually comprise a fifth to a third of the total yield—about five ounces per pound. If the cannabinoid content of the leaf is one-quarter that of the bud, then four ounces have the equivalent potency of nearly an ounce of bud. So for each eleven ounces of bud, there is a "bonus" ounce in the trash. It just has to be collected. The collection and processing of this material is the subject of this book.

The cost of growing marijuana makes bud expensive, even for the grower. So it makes sense to salvage the cannabinoids from the trash. Obviously, it increases the efficiency of one's efforts, but there are other incentives that may attract aficionados to these endeavors.

The reason that leaf products are often called trash is not their low potency. Mexican marijuana often contains similar cannabinoid levels. The problem is the taste and harshness of the smoke, which is rough, acrid and lacking in aroma. No one has developed a method of converting leaf into sweet bud. Instead, most of the techniques described here separate the cannabinoid-bearing glands from the rest of the vegetation. Glands are the only potent part of the plant, so after they are removed, the vegetation can be discarded.

All of the techniques and methods described here have been around for a long time. Some of them were written about in magazines, and others are a part of our heritage. Who hasn't heard of marijuana brownies? The first commercial devices were made in the 1970s and '80s. Why are these techniques developing commercially so many years later?

The reason: prohibition prevents the development of devices that might be used in harm reduction. The Tilt Pipe is an example. It had no other use than to vaporize marijuana. Therefore it was illegal to market. John Gallardi's sifters were ahead of their time too, for the same reason.

Two developments changed the climate. As Europe was moving toward legalization, Mila, located in Holland, invented the Pollinator® and then became involved with bags for making water hash. These two devices and their imitators changed the way large quantities of leaf and trim could be processed. The other development was the ongoing legalization of medical marijuana and devices for its use in states all over the country, beginning with California's Prop. 215 in 1996. Medical marijuana's legal status has spurred creative efforts to meet demand without being thwarted by interference from the states. It could only happen in a legal market. Now we are experiencing sort of a gray market. The states say it's okay, but the federal government maintains its harsh anti-marijuana stance, patients be damned.

During medieval and renaissance periods, alchemists tried to use techniques and spiritual concepts in their unsuccessful quest to turn base metals (lead) to gold. Their quests are generally considered to be the forerunner of modern chemistry. Merlin, the wizard, is a perfect example. He is often depicted wearing an astrological suit and can perform chemical tricks—making smoke or fire. This book furthers the quest of these early experimenters.

Perhaps the main difference between the earlier researchers and modern ones is environmental. People in medieval times lived surrounded by the natural environment and were buffeted daily by the whims of nature. They looked to technology as a magical way to deliver them from the burdens and uncertainties of their lives.

Our lives are controlled more by technology than nature. We have learned how to mitigate many of nature's tricks, at least in the short run. Technology isn't magical, but nature is. The ancients saw technology as complex and nature as simpler, even if inexplicable. Now we know that our most complex devices are simple as compared with the workings of a single cell. We look to nature for our magic and wonder. Rather than seeking gold from the metaphysical transformation of base metals, modern alchemists have turned to base vegetation and found a way to refine its golden portions, the glands and the cannabinoids it contains.

I presume that the reader of this book has used marijuana primarily by burning it and inhaling the smoke. This is only one of the ways it has been used in its long history with humans. It has also been refined, ingested, vaporized, drunk and tinctured. This book explains the wide variety of possible marijuana experiences. Just as alchemists broadened their knowledge and understanding in their quest, the alchemical recipes and techniques in this manual will open new doors of understanding.

1

TRASH BASICS

THC Molecule

CH$_3$

9

OH

H$_3$C

H$_3$C

O

C$_5$H$_{11}$

GARDENERS know that the leaves and trim—the natural byproduct of their work—present an interesting paradox. At 5-15% THC, the bud is the plant's crown jewel, the gardener's reward for attentive caretaking. But cannabis produces THC throughout the plant, not only on the buds. Sticky resin glands coat the leaves and bracts, creating a natural protective barrier against insects, disease, herbivores and the sun's UV rays.

People are familiar with close-up photos of the mushroom-shaped glands on the flowers. Small bulbous or droplet-shaped THC-containing glands are produced on other parts of the plant also. Glands on the leaf and trim contain one-fifth to one-half the THC found in the buds. The fan leaves have a THC content of only 1-3%, so they are a lousy smoke. Trim, with a modest 2-6% THC content, commands only a little more respect than the leaves.

Buds typically weigh twice that of the leaf on a mature female marijuana plant, although this varies tremendously by variety and gardening technique. Still, when trim and leaves are tossed, 10-15% of the plant's total THC production is thrown away. Most gardeners have been content to sacrifice these glands rather than trouble themselves with trying to extract the remaining THC. Sometimes this second-tier material has been used for baking or handed off to grass-poor friends.

Processing the leaf and trim for use as kief, hash, tincture, butter or food requires additional effort that may not seem worth it to a person floating on good weed. It creates another task at harvest time, when there is already a lot of work to be done. Danger of rip-offs or busts may limit the marijuana gardener from adding another step to the harvesting process.

The truth is, deciding to collect and use the trash does not add greatly to the complexity of harvest. Leaves are already being trimmed and bagged; trim from manicuring must already be managed. Being prepared to dry and store this material in advance makes the collection almost as simple as bagging it for the trashcan. Once the trash is saved for use, it only needs to be stored properly. Transforming the leaves and trim into stash can wait until the rush of harvest is complete.

There are many tools available to simplify turning trash into stash. New products and technology have invented easier ways to process this secondary material, creating a renaissance of cannabis consumables. The resurgence of marijuana medical use has also generated interest in alternatives to smoking.

This book offers traditional methods and recent innovations for processing leaf and trim into worthwhile stash.

A little information combined with some simple equipment not only maximizes the harvest, but also takes full advantage of marijuana's many uses.

This is a great book if you are interested in alternatives to smoking as a connoisseur or medical user. The pages that follow will provide you with some of the simplest, easiest and safest ways to turn your trash into stash.

KNOW YOUR TRASH/COLLECT FOR STASH

When tossing it out, trash is everything that isn't bud. When saving trash with an eye to transforming it, the recycler may want to be more discerning. Stems and woody parts of the plant are not salvageable. The sticks dry more slowly than the leaves, and their moisture may spoil the useable material by causing it to mold.

Aside from branch and stem parts, the main factor that sorts good trash from bad is the ratio of THC in the material. Tetrahydrocannabinol (THC), the main psychoactive component of marijuana, as well as other cannabinoids that give each variety a characteristic high, are produced on the stems, leaves and vegetation surrounding the flowers, and stored in glands that emerge from the surface.

Grades of Trash

The flowering areas of the female plants and the small leaves surrounding them contain the most THC—from twice to five times as much as other parts of the plant. However, all the leaves from the mature female plant contain retrievable THC. Male plants contain THC as well, and are most potent at the budding but pre-flowering stage. In both cases, the small leaves near the flowers are the most potent, followed by the younger and then older fan leaves.

It may be useful to get a magnifying glass or photographer's loupe and take a close-up look at the plant material. The glands on the fan leaves are often small and hug the surface of the leaf, while the glands near the flowers are stalked and look like mushrooms with bulbous caps. Material with visible glands is worth keeping. While immature material can also be collected, it is best to use trash that has been collected from mature plants to get the intended results. In a recycling effort, a gardener may opt to trash material with the sparsest glands, such as the large fan leaves, while saving the smaller leaves, trim and bud bits for use.

THE TRASH HIERARCHY
Trash can be divided into several categories. This list prioritizes salvageable trash according to its THC content:

1. Bud bits and pieces, or cosmetically challenged "popcorn bud"
2. Bag shake: the residue at the bottom of the bag
3. Primary trim: the small leaves near the bud sites
4. Mature fan leaves: the large sun leaves
5. Immature buds: these will vary in THC content depending on stage of maturity
6. Immature trim/immature leaf: also variable depending on stage of development
5. Vegetative leaf: leaf from a plant that has not entered flowering phase of growth; has the lowest THC content

At minimum, the woody parts of the plant should be sorted out of the useable material and thrown away. It is best to separate the trash into two rough categories of higher and lower quality. Large fan leaves should be separated from the higher potency trim. Further divisions are possible: for instance, small "popcorn" bud pieces may also be sorted from the trim and bagged separately. After ditching the stems and woody parts, the remaining material can be sorted either while the plant is being manicured, or after being dried.

GLANDS AND QUALITY

The cannabinoids and THC are contained in the glands, and not all glands are created equal. Glands vary for several reasons, including the growing technique and the plant's genetics.

- On some plants, the gland itself is actually bigger than on other plants. Larger glands hold more resin.
- Strains also vary in how concentrated the crystallization is. Some plants may have smaller glands, but in large numbers that carpet the plant. Some varieties are more prone to produce a lot of vegetation, which means more gland-bearing leaf and trim to transform.
- Resin quality also varies. Obviously the quality of the resin affects the quality of the product. If a variety of marijuana is not very potent, then concentrating the glands will create a mediocre concentrate. Schwag weed has lower potency and therefore may not produce the same quality of product as high-quality weed.

Most processes start by separating the glands or cannabinoids from the plant material. Concentrating the psychoactive components results in a more intense high since the potency is increased. These may make a better high from lesser quality weed. However, if you started with quality weed the product will obviously be more potent.

Sophisticated growers often keep their trash separated by variety, just as they do with their buds. The quality of high associated with inhaling different varieties carries over to other methods of ingestion.

Each method in the book may suggest which trash is most suitable to use to get good results. For instance, vaporizing uses high-grade trash, such as bud bits or "popcorn bud," but this trash isn't the most suitable for all methods. Some high bakers say that "buds are for smoking not for cooking" and find that the food products turn out better when mostly trim and leaf is used as described in that chapter. Still, if you are going for a certain stash product in the book, or you want to only save the most valuable trash, then it is possible to sort by the grades suggested on p. 8.

STORING THE GREEN

After the trash is collected, it should be dried until crisp. It is important for the material to dry thoroughly because the THC molecule is fairly inactive in the plant with a water molecule attached to it. When the plant dries out, the THC and other cannabinoids release the water and become active.

DRYING THE HARVEST   ASK ED

Ed:
What is the correct way of drying plant clippings?
Courtney,
Las Vegas, Nevada

Courtney:
In Las Vegas, where it is very dry, the buds and leaves dry out quickly if left out on a warm autumn day. If the grass is dried outdoors it should be kept in the dark or deeply shaded area since light and heat destroy THC. Line the clippings thinly on a cookie sheet, cardboard, newspaper or other flat surface. Turn it several times if it is drying unevenly.

Indoors, there are several ways to dry the leaves. The trays of leaves can be placed in a space at room temperature with a draft from an open window. Leaves and trim can be loosely bagged in paper grocery bags and set in a cool, dark area that has some airflow. In moist areas the trim and leaf can be placed in a food dehydrator on a low setting, or they can be dried in an enclosed space with a dehumidifier.

Several methods can be used for drying. Some people lay the material out flat on newspaper or screens and wait for it to dry, then bag it in plastic storage bags. If dealing with large quantities, or in particularly humid areas, a fan or dehumidifier can be run in the drying area, but it isn't essential. If there's no room to spread out the material, one easy method that is equally good is to fill paper bags half-full with material, and set them in an out-of-the-way place that gets some air flow. The bags will allow enough circulation to draw out moisture. Finally, an electric food dehydrator set on low heat can speed or complete the drying process.

When stored in a cool dry area, dried material can be kept for several years with little deterioration. Of course, there is no problem storing material in areas with low humidity, such as the dry southwest.

The cannabinoids are destroyed in the presence of light and heat, especially around oxygen. The best possible way to preserve cannabis is to store it in the dark at a cool to cold temperature in an oxygen-free environment. It will keep for long periods when it is stored in sealed, opaque containers in a cool place.

In areas with high humidity, moisture may get into the material after it has dried. This causes rot, indicated by an ammonia odor; or mold, indicated by gray or white growth on the leaves. In either case, the pot gets ruined. One way to keep the greenery wholesome until it is used is to keep it in a frost-free refrigerator or a freezer once it's dried. These appliances preserve the dryness and stop any deterioration of THC. The material can also be dried to crispness and then placed in plastic bags or Seal-A-Meals. The material will stay fresh until you are ready to use it.

TIPS & TRICKS
THE ALCHEMY OF MARIJUANA PROCESSING

There are a few common rules to processing marijuana that will be mentioned throughout. These simple principles about the chemical nature and limits of marijuana are important for understanding how to process the plant material to result in a quality product.

Solubility

THC is not water soluble; it is soluble in oils, fats and alcohol. The tinctures and foods presented in the book are extracts of THC from trim or leaves using alcohol, butter or oil as the solvent.

Assimilation

Assimilation refers to the time it takes for cannabis to have an effect after it is used. Another aspect of assimilation is the quantity that is required to reach a certain state of highness. Different methods of intake are assimilated with varied efficiency. Smoking, vaporizing, tinctures and eating each produce a distinct high.

The benefit of quick assimilation is that it is easier to figure out how much to use. Smoking or vaporizing has a fast onset, so you know quickly whether or not you have a sufficient dose.

Ingesting tinctures sublingually—that is, droplets placed under the tongue—is an intermediate between smoking and eating. It is not as fast as smoking or vaporizing, but it does not have to pass through the digestive system. Within five minutes after the tincture is dropped on the tongue, effects are felt.

Drinking or eating cannabis has a much slower onset and the effects of a particular dose will vary.

12

One of the most important factors is whether cannabized food is eaten on an empty or full stomach. On an empty stomach the food is digested both more efficiently and faster. The high starts coming on after 20-30 minutes and peaks at about two to three hours. The high is intense with several peaks and lasts four hours or more. On a full stomach, the high begins 45-60 minutes after ingestion and peaks three to four hours after ingestion. It may last six or seven hours; however, it is not as intense.

While the high can be enjoyable and long lasting, it is harder to determine the right amount to use for the high you want. The feedback loop can take up to four hours. As a result it is easier to eat more or less than intended and end up with a too-heady buzz, or not much of a buzz at all.

Dosage

Assimilation has a range from person to person that, unlike alcohol, is not entirely attributable to a person's weight or metabolism. Other factors may make what is not enough for one person too much for another.

Trying to distinguish between marijuana's psychoactive and therapeutic effects is difficult. It is also difficult to establish a consistent dosage through all methods of intake. When the same material is used and the same processes are followed, this is somewhat easier to determine. Caution should always be used when trying out a new variety or a new technique for processing. It may take a little careful experimentation to find the right amount, and the amount that is right for you may not be the same for someone else.

2

VAPORIZERS

SMOKING is one of the most controversial aspects of cannabis use. Scientific studies have shown that marijuana releases tars and other potentially harmful compounds when burned. While marijuana can have positive effects, common sense suggests that smoking is bad for the lungs.

Using marijuana for medical benefit has raised new concerns about this contradiction. Since THC and the other cannabinoids don't pose any health hazards, but the tars and other compounds may, people have sought out alternate modes of ingestion. Cooking and tinctures have been around for centuries, but their delivery, onset and effects are different than smoked marijuana. History proves that even people who enjoy marijuana in food or tinctures are unlikely to quit smoking pot entirely in favor of these forms.

Enter the vaporizer. The vaporizer is a fantastic innovation. It works because the temperature at which THC and other cannabinoids evaporate is lower than the temperature at which plant material burns. This device allows marijuana to be inhaled without the tars or other harmful compounds released from burning plant material.

Preliminary studies suggest that vaporizers reduce the health risks associated with smoking. Vaporizing may also be a more efficient use of cannabis. When marijuana is burned, up to 30% of the THC content is lost to the combustion process. Since vaporizers evaporate the THC without combusting the plant material, it is possible to get more THC from the same amount of weed.

The vaporizer concept has actually been around for some time. The first known device that worked by vaporizing marijuana was introduced in 1979 under the name "the Tilt." This short-lived device was doomed to obscurity by the passage of anti-paraphernalia laws in the early 1980s.

In 1994, BC Vaporizers manufactured prototype models of a device and named it "the Vaporizer." The name stuck, and is now used generically to refer to all of the various vapor devices. Many inventor-types in Europe, Canada and the U.S have emerged since the mid-1990s, flooding the market with choices. This chapter explains how they work and reviews the different types of vaporizers currently available.

HOW VAPORIZERS WORK

Vaporizers capitalize on the fact that THC transforms into a vapor at a lower temperature than the temperature at which plant material burns. Just like water can be turned into vapor, THC resin can be turned from a liquid to a gas without actually combusting the plant material.

Some vaporizers are designed to resemble familiar paraphernalia. There are bong-like models and a few portable types that are similar to pipes. Favorite bongs can even be adapted for vaporization techniques. Other models look like foreign gadgetry. All vaporizers involve a heating element, a bowl-like part that holds the marijuana, and a way of catching and drawing the vapor.

Vaporizers generally require more presence of mind to operate than your standard bong or waterpipe. Some models are designed to be mobile or easy to use, but learning to operate a vaporizer takes a little adjustment.

The Vaporizer High

The first time you use a vaporizer, it may seem odd. You inhale air that has the faintly suggestive odor of cannabis, but there is no smoke. It doesn't quite feel the same. The harshness and flavor of the smoke is noticeably absent. It may even feel like nothing is happening. And then, suddenly, it dawns on you that you're high.

The high may also feel different than when smoking. Some people report that they get stoned quickly when using a vaporizer. Others note that the high seems to be lighter or more head-oriented. If the vaporization temperature was reached slowly, the presence of other cannabinoids may produce a sleepy high.

Many medical marijuana patients prefer the vaporizer because its delivery is as rapid as smoking, but without the unwanted tars. Some smokers adjust easily to vaporization, but others report that the high produced from vaporizing lacks something more than just the smoke. This may be the result of poor vaporizer performance or

17

vaporization technique. It could be partly psychological. Smokers are conditioned to anticipate the high when they taste and feel the smoke. Vaporizing and smoking are both complex chemical exchanges of marijuana's nearly 500 constituents. It seems completely reasonable that they produce subtly different experiences.

Vaporizer Mechanics

A little knowledge helps to ensure an enjoyable and healthy vaporizing experience. There are a few key mechanics that determine a good vaporizer.

The first is heat. Vaporizers are designed to maintain a temperature that is safely within a specific range. THC's boiling point is 392 degrees F (200 degrees C), but active vapors form at almost 100 degrees lower. Marijuana's active components turn to vapor between 260-392 degrees F. The ideal temperature for vaporization is subject to debate, but is usually suggested in the range 330-375 degrees F. Smoke begins to form at temperatures over 360 degrees F. When the temperature goes over the 400-degree mark, tars and other undesirable compounds such as benzene and dioxins are released. When ignited, the temperature soars to 600 degrees F or higher.

Vaporizer heating elements must maintain a stable temperature to produce vapor without burning the plant material. Many vaporizer models are designed to reach the desired temperature range quickly. There is a solid scientific reason for this as well. Since THC and the other cannabinoids vaporize at slightly different temperatures, rapid heating delivers the full cannabinoid spectrum simultaneously.

Some vaporizers allow the user to control the temperature, while others are designed to reach the correct temperature without any adjustable settings. The latter models are convenient because they avoid the learning curve, but they lose some flexibility in the process. An adjustable model adds complexity to the process, and only contributes to the design when the basic principles of vaporization are understood. Gaining mastery over the temperature controls takes a little time and experimentation.

Two types of temperature control are common. The heating element may have settings, allowing the user to monitor the exact temperature. Once the right setting is determined, it only needs occasional, minute adjustments.

Moving the bowl to control the temperature is more intuitive, and involves some coordination while drawing a hit. This may seem like a downside, but it has one advantage. The temperature is determined not only by the heating element, but also by the strength of a person's draw. A strong inhale will cause the temperature to spike. After adjusting the heat for such a user, a person who inhales lightly may not draw hard enough to get a decent hit. Many vaporizer inventors recommend slow, even, meditative breaths for inhaling vapor.

When vaporizing, the bowl should expose the greatest possible surface area of the material to the heat source. Greater surface area means more available resin to evaporate. The bowl should also keep the bud at an even distance from the heat source. Uneven application of heat will cause the hotter area to burn or toast, which may produce smoke and will alter the taste. The cooler parts will rest in the bowl with the resin intact.

Well-designed models have a small vapor collection area. By the time the vapor is inhaled, its temperature has begun to drop. This is better for the lungs, since hot, dry air is unhealthy, even when it doesn't contain smoke.

However, as the cannabinoids cool, they condense into dew. Large collection areas provide more surfaces to which the dew can cling, making it irretrievable.

Because high temperatures are involved, all materials used to build a vaporizer should be safe when heated. Copper and aluminum release toxic fumes at the temperatures needed for vaporization. Models containing these metals create a health hazard and should not be used. Glass, stainless steel, and brass are all safe materials.

PREPARING HERB FOR VAPORIZING

Bud is used for vaporizing. Salvaged bud bits work well because the material is ground before it is used. Kief or crumbled hash can also be vaporized. All vaporizers also work with other medicinal herbs.

Grinding the bud improves the flow of air and maximizes the surface area that is exposed to heat. A coarse grind is best. In chamber-type models, kief is easily used by itself. In other models, fine material is layered on top of coarsely ground material to avoid clogging up the works.

Grinders make quick work of preparing the bud. These totally manual, pocket-sized disks are simply filled and twisted to reduce the material. The consistency is determined by the amount of time the material is ground. Bud can also be reduced by rubbing it against a wire mesh kitchen strainer over a collection tray.

It is better to use freshly ground buds, but if there is some extra after grinding, place it in an airtight container and store it in a dark, cool place.

SWEETLEAF™ GRINDERS

Vaporizers achieve the best results when the herb is finely ground. Fortunately there's a simple solution. Grinders . . . they're everywhere, in all sizes, shapes, materials and colors. We all have Sweetleaf™ to thank for the flood of grinders available today.

The original Sweetleaf™ grinder rolled onto the market in the late 1990s. The first product of its kind, this pocket-sized disk of beautifully lathed hardwood was a smooth little timesaver that caught on quickly. In 2001, it took first place at the Cannabis Cup for best product (non-hemp). Sweetleaf™ grinders are now available in two sizes in either the original wood or tooled aluminum. All models are small enough to fit in your pocket, yet large enough to do the job.

Just place the herb inside, join the pieces together, and then twist until the herb is the consistency you want. The pins do the work. These hand-powered grinders let you determine the grind: coarser for pipe smoking, or finer for vaporizing. They work with a variety of herbs, and can also be used to prepare material for other processes, such as kief making.

Sweetleaf™ is a family-owned business based in Toronto, Canada. Their grinders range between $15-$30, and are available internationally. See the resource section at the end of the chapter for contact information.

THE VAPORIZERS

All vaporizer models work from the same set of scientific principles. The following descriptions and reviews are intended to give a basic overview of the main types of vaporizers currently available.

The review process has been a group effort. Some vaporizer inventors and designers offered information and

21

demonstrations of their products. Our "Tester" has compiled information and reviews from a panel of anonymous connoisseurs and experts, who personally tested each model for ease of use and quality of results. Thanks to all who contributed to the development of this chapter.

At the end of the chapter, a resource section lists information on all of the models discussed here, plus several vaporizers that were unavailable for review. All prices listed are in U.S. dollars unless otherwise indicated.

The BC Vaporizer™
$65-$75 (Canadian)
Heat element: conduction through brass bowl (options: electricity or 12-volt car-adaptor)

With over 30,000 models sold, this pioneer in the field of vaporization is a simple chamber device that has undergone several design improvements since its prototype was developed in 1994.

The BC Vaporizer™ has a small chamber with a brass bowl where the bud is placed. The bowl heats the marijuana, and the collected vapor is drawn through flexible tubing. There are no adjustments on this device. The temperature is automatically controlled and reaches a maximum temperature of 572 degrees F.

The model comes in one piece that is a convenient size, about 4-5 inches wide and 7 inches tall. There are no exposed heating elements. When running, the vaporizer gets slightly warm but is comfortable to hold in the hand. The glass top screws off for reloading and cleaning.

This model is available in 110-volt and 220-volt models. Twelve-volt car adaptors are also available.

BC Vaporizer™ Review

Tester was happy to see this vaporizer come out of the box in one piece . . . no extra parts or bits to juggle or keep track of. The fellow making the BC Vaporizer™ is a plastic smith, and it shows in the simple, artistic design. Take it out and plug it in . . . that's all you do! Once the unit heats up, place a small amount of material on the brass "dish" and put the glass top on. Vapor collects in the glass top and is drawn out through a hookah-like tube. Tester found this to be a nice vaporizer for socializing. It's easy to pass around within a small group at a table and is like a hookah, in that sharing way.

Tester burned some material, but thinks it happened because the material was left in too long and over-zealously sucked at while Tester yammered on about something or another. Practice and familiarity with this vaporizer (and Tester believes this is applicable to all vaporizers) are essential. Overall, Tester enjoyed this well-designed, easy-to-use, low-hassle vaporizer. There are many companies making chamber-style vaporizers, and price can vary greatly. Be sure the company doesn't use copper for the bowl (unless you like lead fumes). BC Vaporizers are well made, safe and have years of development and research to back them up.

The Eterra Tulip™

$122, Replacement stems: **$12-20**
Heat element: reverse convection capacitor (requires electricity)

The Eterra Tulip™ is a metal cone with a tulip heater secured within. The pipe parts are made of brass and stainless steel. Three types of "hot boot" stems of different sizes fit the Eterra™, and replacements can be bought separately. The vaporizer takes about 10 minutes to heat up and is thereafter ready when you are. It draws only about 7-8 watts of power.

The Tulip's heater uses high-tech ceramics to completely seal the heating element for safe, non-toxic vaporizing. A specially designed double coil uses reverse convection to deliver a precise temperature between 340-360 degrees F. It is the first device to employ this heating technique, which allows for the conveniently compact size.

In some models, the pot is held so that it may cook at the bottom, but stay cool on top. The Tulip's bowl inserts so that it is all covered and exposed to heat evenly. This also preserves the material because less is lost to the air.

The heat is adjusted by the human sense of taste and temperature. Inhaling draws the warmed air inside the Tulip™ over the heat sink, superheating it so that it vaporizes at the correct temperature in seconds. It can burn if drawn on too long. The breath control is fairly easy to intuit. When the vapor coming into your mouth feels warm, stop inhaling. If you find it difficult to sense the temperature, use time as a gauge, inserting the stem for about 5-6 seconds. Vapor is still forming when the stem is removed from the heat source. Continue to inhale. This can be the most flavorful and satisfying time. The stem can be reinserted for another round.

The Tulip™ inventor is currently working on a cordless model that will operate on battery power.

Eterra Tulip™ Review

This compact vaporizer is both easy to use and looks like industrial art. Tester likes the way it fits into the hand, is warm to the touch and is low hassle. Tester would like to repeat this important fact—the Tulip™ is a no-hassle vaporizer that fits into the palm of your hand. Ground herb is loosely packed into a receiver that is then inserted into the Tulip™. Vapor is drawn out, but the receiver is never left in the Tulip™ for extended periods. Many small hits can be taken off a surprisingly small amount of herb. The "smoked" herb can then be emptied into a small cloth bag (provided). The used herb has a pleasing smell and can be used later for herbal remedies.

Each Tulip™ has an LED light inside. The colors vary but the overall effect is the same . . . it's fun to look at. Plus, it's helpful to know if the power is on. The receiving hole and the small area around it get very hot. Always make sure loose papers, cloth and other flammables are kept away from the unit.

Tester took this vaporizer on a weekend trip to a house on a river. The Tulip™ was plugged in all weekend with a bowl of ground herb next to it as an added incentive to experiment and learn. It was man-handled, dropped twice, passed around, used like a groupie and never complained. Even so, Tester couldn't recruit some old heads to change teams. They would courteously accept Tester's offers of vapor hits, and then smoke a bowl when Tester's attention wandered or Tester wandered off.

Tester has tried many vaporizers, and all have a learning curve. Of all the units tested, the Tulip™ is the easiest to use, most low profile, affordable, safe and hassle-free system yet.

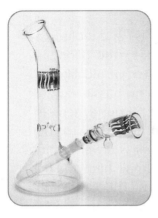

Vrip Tech™ 007 Kit
$420 on website
(regular retail price: $600)
Includes: top-of-the-line heat gun, high-impact plastic case, all necessary glass wear, file. **$50** Bowl only. Bong, heat guns and replacement parts can also be bought separately. **Heat element:** heat gun (requires electricity)

The Vrip Tech™ Vaporizer is modeled after a bong, allowing the user to keep the ritual sans the smoke. In 1999, this vaporizer won the silver medal for best product at the Cannabis Cup.

You can get the whole ball of wax, the "007 kit," or just buy the special vaporization chamber bowl and fit it to your own favorite bong. If you don't get the complete kit, you'll also need a heat gun, which is available through Vrip Tech™ or most hardware stores.

The Vrip Tech™ vaporization chamber bowl is a tightly tooled 2-piece glass set with two o-rings at the joints. The o-ring can be filed down for a smoother fitting. The bottom glass piece looks like a regular bong bowl. This piece is loaded with material, and then fitted inside the second piece of glass, which looks kind of like a shot glass with the bottom removed. The funnel shape—going from wider to narrower as it reaches the bowl—is a special design that takes advantage of the laws of gases: It uses the Venturi effect to increase the efficiency of the heat used. The gun fits into the end of the shot glass piece.

The bong is filled with either a combination of water and ice, or just with ice. You might think the ice is for cooling, what with a 300+ degree gun going into the end. Cooling is secondary. The ice's main purpose is to take up space that would otherwise be taken up by air. Ice and water help to create a more vacuum-like atmosphere, with less oxygen to degrade your fine pot.

The heat gun setting controls the heat level. The Vrip Tech™ heat guns have a thermostat regulator. The gun attempts to maintain the temperature at which it is set. Even breaths help to maintain a constant temperature. It is good to run the heat gun's fan on the lowest setting to avoid driving more air into the vapor than necessary. The gun's controls can be taped at the best settings once they are determined, which prevents them from being changed or accidentally bumped up or down in the middle of vaporizing.

Vrip Tech™ inventor McCoy is currently working on portable and mini models. He's also looking for other effective ways to run the heating element to eliminate the need for the cumbersome heat gun.

Vrip Tech™ Review

Talk about fancy packaging! Tester was blown away by this sophisticated set-up. Tester did feel like a 007 agent when first opening the high-impact, plastic case in front of friends. Each piece has its own fitted spot in the heat-resistant foam interior, and there's room to put your stash jar. Plus, there are two places to throw on a padlock for the paranoid. All the fittings are sold separately, in case you just need a replacement piece or only want the bowl and stem to use with your favorite water pipe.

Tester cleared the table, plugged in the heat gun, loaded the glass chamber with water and ice, gathered the friends and put on some old-timey music. The heat gun in this kit has a digital temperature readout Tester found to be very helpful and accurate. Tester burned no material with this unit.

Tester wants everyone to know that the high was fantastic from this vaporizer. It rated tops in taste. As a novelty, it was even possible to drink the usually feared bongwater, which tasted like a mild, exotic tea. Tester had fun using the product, reading the included information and adding a bit more ceremony to the usual ritual. While Tester appreciated the fact that this vaporizer worked like it was supposed to, it was also time consuming and involved. Call Tester old-fashioned, resistant to change, and ill tempered. It won't change the fact that Tester could have been ripped and out the door in less than half the time if fire had been used.

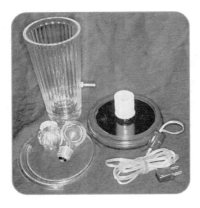

The PotCooker™
$36 assembled
Free directions to make
your own on website
Heat element: light bulb
(requires electricity)

The PotCooker™ is a low-cost, low-tech vaporizer that uses a heavy-duty acrylic drinking tumbler as a collection chamber over a circular, footed wooden base that has a high-quality porcelain light bulb socket. A bowl is fashioned on 60-watt ceiling fan light bulb, which acts as the heating source. Food-grade clear vinyl tubing is attached near the top of the tumbler with a brass fitting.

The system instructs the user to mold a bowl atop the light bulb using aluminum foil; however, aluminum is not recommended since it produces ions when heated. The user will have to make this risk assessment. Other makeshift bowls might be easily fashioned from safer materials.

PotCooker™ Review

You say you don't have $100 to $400 to drop on a fancy vaporizer? Well, the folks at Potcooker.com are willing to give you free directions to make your own vaporizer for a few bucks, or sell you an assembled one for less than $40. Tester thought this was pretty unbelievable too, so invited a representative from PotCooker.com over to show off the product.

Huh . . . a plastic cup put over a light bulb covered in tinfoil? It does make a serviceable vaporizer. Who knew? The folks at PotCooker.com apparently did. A small amount of herb is set onto the tinfoil "bowl," the light bulb is switched on, the cup is set over the bulb and viola, you're sucking vapor through a tube.

The only concern Tester had about this vaporizer is the use of tinfoil as a bowl. Tester is sure aluminum foil emits toxic vapors, but at what temperature? Tester remembers all the times aluminum foil came through as a screen in a pinch.

Tester enjoyed this creative, yet simply designed tool. As far as vaporizers go, it's easy to use, has few breakable parts and can be put together for a few bucks. Tester didn't go the whole nine yards and make the PotCooker™ from scratch, but the directions on the web site look easy to follow.

The Volcano™
$499 on website
(regular retail price: $799)
Heat element: internal
membrane-pump heat
dispenser (requires electricity)

This vaporizer comes from an Austrian company named Vapomed. The stainless steel "volcano" shaped console is made of stainless steel and is about 10 inches at the base.

29

A chamber fits into the two-inch top. A heavy-duty, food-grade plastic bag (turkey bag) attaches to a final piece, which clips to the chamber. The temperature is controlled with a dial on the front of the machine. A light on the front indicates when the heat is clicked to the on position (like a light switch). The red light turns off again when the proper temperature is reached.

Once the heating element is ready, a second switch turns on the air, which pumps the plastic bag full of vapor. The bag is removed from the base once it has filled. It has a pressure-controlled mouthpiece that releases the vapor. Models are designed in European voltage, but converters for U.S. use are available.

Volcano™ Review

The shiny, one-piece Volcano chamber looked very promising. At the price, Tester was glad to find that everything but the bud came with this system, including the plastic baggies and a very detailed set of instructions on using it.

This model was very easy to operate. The black, hard plastic chamber is similar to a coffee press, with a short rod that fits on top to hold the weed. The clip-on parts were easy to attach and detach. The temperature seemed to work best when set at 7 or 8. It was possible for Tester to produce smoke with this model, but adjusting the temperature control was simple and non-scary. It was pleasant to have a light indicator. This made the heating phase hands-free, and it was clear when the device was ready to use.

The Volcano™ can be left running with no air flow for ten minutes without burning the pot, even on the highest heat setting (which, by the way, is higher than you need to vaporize). Of course, Tester recommends turning it off when it is unattended or not in use.

With a flick of the switch, the air flow is on and filling the bag. This is the main part that needs to be monitored.

Best of all is the detachable bag. It can be passed around easily with no cords to worry about, and it weighs practically nothing. The mouthpiece works like some water bottle tops do. Pressing against it releases the vapor. The bag can be easily refilled 2-3 times from the same bowl.

Tester's only concerns were that the vapor should not be left in the bag for long, since the THC quality will diminish. The bag also allows a lot of surface area for condensation.

Still, Tester could imagine that this model is very practical for many medical users, especially when mobility is an issue. Operating the Volcano™ requires no lifting and the only coordination needed is in loading the pot and unclipping the bag. The hot parts are all enclosed in the base, making the inhalation balloon totally safe to handle or set down on any surface. The bag can be used from any position: standing, sitting or laying down.

The Vapor Cannon™
$135, Replacement parts: **$16-25**
Heat element: iron conduction element (requires electricity)

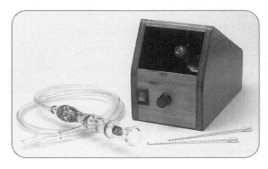

The Vapor Cannon™ consists of a wooden box that contains the heat element, and a piece of flexible tubing with Pyrex™ glass pieces on both ends. The larger glass piece is the bowl, and the smaller piece is the drawing end.

The knob on the front of the heat console adjusts the temperature. There are no markings around the knob, but turning it clockwise increases the heat level. The console is plugged in and turned to maximum temperature, and then moved back about 1/8 to 1/4 to achieve proper vaporization. It takes 2-3 minutes to heat up and should glow a dim red when it is at the proper temperature.

A thin layer of prepared bud is placed in the screen inside the wand-like bowl. When ready to inhale, touch the bowl piece to the iron element on the console and draw through the other end of the tube. The temperature is controlled by both the strength of the draw and the heat level of the iron element. This machine requires two hands to operate.

When the exhale gives off a thin bluish smoke, the bud is spent. The bowl is emptied by blowing through the tube while holding the bowl over an ashtray or trashcan.

The screen's gentle placement inside the glass tube may be accidentally pushed out of place. It is a little tricky to get it back in place, but a tool that accompanies the Vapor Cannon™ is meant to assist with screen replacement. When loaded and emptied with care, the screen should stay in place and last.

The tubing should be cleaned out with a hot water rinse every few weeks to avoid clogging. A 220-volt model for European use will be available soon.

VaporCannon™ Review

At first glance, Tester wasn't sure about the Vapor Cannon™ design. The temperature control knob seemed encouraging, but the console's hot end pointed slightly upward, and the glass tube with the herb in it pointed downward when drawing air, defying gravity.

The first step involves sucking a small amount of herb into the tube. It can be lightly tamped against the screen with the tool provided. (The screen looks like it may come loose but is in the receiver quite snugly.) The glass end is applied to the hot top, and air is drawn through. The receiving tube with the herb is removed from heat, and the remaining vapors are drawn through.

Tester worried about the glass parts connected to the tube. They looked strong and durable, but still, they were made of glass. Tester knows about glass—it breaks. Fortunately the company sells replacement parts.

All of Tester's design-flaw worries were thrown out the window after the first 20 minutes. It does take time to learn to adjust the temperature to the desired degree; despite that small learning curve, Tester never burned the herb and always got a great hit. Only a few of the vaporizers made it through the first test toke without burning the bud. Tester thinks this says a lot about the product. The Vapor Cannon™ is easy to use. Since it doesn't even look like a vaporizer, it is also a stealth piece of paraphernalia.

Basic White and Citrus Air2™
VAPIR™ Digital Air Kit

$299. Includes: world adaptor (100V-240V), small custom-fit protective case, 2 empty herb disks, user's manual, small plastic tool. Replacement herb disks: **10 for $19.99.** Supercharger: **$199,** Car adaptor: **$99.** Custom shoulder pack: **$49.99**
Heat element: internal ceramic heater (options: electricity, battery or 12-volt car-adaptor)

The word *digital* in the name of this product should be the first clue that it is based on advanced technology. An impressive crew of engineers and professionals were recruited to develop this portable, state-of-the-art device. This system uses a digital microchip and has USB interface capabilities.

The Vapir™ looks like a handheld kitchen blender. The internal ceramic heater works by convection to heat the herbal matter. Flexible tubing is attached at the top of the device, forming a vapor straw. An herbal "disk drive" resembles a tea strainer. When inserted, it is completely enclosed in the machine. A viewing window at the top of the device allows the user to monitor the amount of smoke being produced.

The bottom half of the device has digital controls for the temperature and air settings. An LCD readout displays the temperature. The included instruction manual explains how to operate these digital controls. The learning curve on this machine is higher than other models, but the technology is intended to offer very precise control once mastered.

Vapir™ Review

Tester was fascinated by the shiny backpack this vaporizer arrived in . . . very hip, over-one-shoulder design. There's nothing like gadgets, cords, small shiny things and cool packaging to get a Head interested.

The promise of a future USB port upgrade sent the Tester on a wild journey of imagination and speculation long before any herb was sampled.

Once out of the package, plugged in and on the table, Tester opened the instruction booklet to get the 411. To be honest, Tester tried to make it go without reading the directions. Tester found the directions to be key in the initial operation of this vaporizer. They are smartly laid out in a clear, easy-to-understand manner.

At this point Tester is confident (having read the directions) and eager to get started while the unit is warming up to burn off any dust or residue built up by non-use. Tester has ground up herb and put it in the basket, adjusted the temperature, recruited a friend and fuddled with everything that came in the kit.

Herb disk is inserted, cycle begins and the faintest sweet herb smell begins to come from the tube. Smoke-tinged vapor suddenly begins pouring out of the tube at an alarming rate; the fan is pumping the vapor out too fast!

Alarmed, Tester and friend begin passing the unit back and forth faster and faster, overwhelmed by the amount of vapor. Suddenly, smoke is pouring out of everywhere. Tester manually turns the temperature down, then decides to abort this attempt and start over at a lower temperature. Tester found removing the herb disk to be a hassle . . . after allowing the unit's fan to run to cool the receiver for the herb disk, it was still very hot. The herb in the center of the disk was burned.

After turning the temperature down and reloading the herb disk, Tester and friend watched through the window to wait for vapor to build up. The "laser lights" were supposed to help us see. Smoke again began pouring from everywhere and Tester turned the power off. The unit itself was not smoking; it was the herb in the disk.

Tester found the best way to get a good vaporizer hit from this unit was to preheat the unit to desired temperature before inserting the herb disk. Once the unit is heated, open it and insert the disk. Tester then inhaled vapor and was done before the herb burned. The herb always burned, making Tester wonder if this unit was designed for cannabis use, and wondering how reliable the temperature setting on the heat element is.

Overall, Tester found the packaging, presentation, marketing and aesthetics of this vaporizer to be fantastic, but those can't make up for function, affordability, and performance.

Cool Vapors™

Contact company for pricing. Heat element: Electric coil element

The Cool Vapors™ device has two distinct parts: A console with two coil-type (car) cigarette lighters mounted in it, and a special sliding glass bowl. The bowl can be used on its own as a smokeless cigarette, much like a one-hitter, or it can serve as a stem for any standard bong. Small waterpipes can be bought from Cool Vapors™ as a part of the system.

The console has an on/off switch with a light indicator. The lighters are an easy heat source to figure out. They pop up when hot and can be repeatedly reheated for continuous vaporization.

The sliding glass bowl is constructed with an interior piece that houses the bowl. A larger, test-tube-like piece fits over the top, encasing the loaded bowl. A black rubber fitting allows the top piece to be adjusted so that the heat source is held at a proper distance from the material to create a vapor without burning. As the coil element cools, the sliding tube can be pushed closer to the bowl to control the heat.

The breath intake also controls the vapor production. Since the vapor is drawn just like a usual bong hit, and the bowl adjustment is similar to how a bowl is adjusted when smoking, most bong users can easily adapt and operate the Cool Vapors™ system intuitively.

CoolVapors™ Review

Such a peculiar heating device: a black box with two car lighters side by side that spring from the top. Tester thinks this console looks like a chess timer, and could double as a cigarette lighter at parties. Also included is a sliding glass herb receiver. The glass receiver can be used like a cigarette or double as a replacement vaporizer stem for a favorite bong or waterpipe. If using the herb receiver as a cigarette without the waterpipe, the "cigarette" portion can be quickly hidden and all that remains visible to prying eyes is the innocuous "chess timer/party lighter." A small waterpipe is available for purchase from Cool Vapors™ to complete the set.

Tester read the instructions, warmed up the "chess timer" and pulled up a comfy chair. A small amount of herb went into the receiver, and the stem was pulled back to create a buffer zone from the heat. The receiver's stem was inserted in the bong and the first lighter popped up on the "chess timer."

The heat from the lighter coil doesn't last long and the best hit will be when it's freshly "popped." Tester inhaled deeply while applying the coil to the glass tip, and all seemed to go well. The herb was flipped over in the bowl to expose the unheated side and Tester took another go at it. Burned it to a crisp, Tester did. Agh, the learning curve comes free with the purchase of every vaporizer.

Once you're acquainted with this system, it is easy to use and low profile. The multi-purpose design is a plus. Tester tried the Cool Vapors™ waterpipe style and cigarette style. Tester liked it both ways and is ready for a game of chess.

**Eagle Bill's
Shake 'N Vap™**
$22.95
Heat element: flame

Eagle Bill was among the original vapor pioneers. He became known in parts of Europe, where he wandered on his pilgrimage for vaporization techniques. He is among the few inventors who have designed simple, portable vapor pipes.

This model looks like a slightly strange glass pipe. It has no built-in heating device. Ground bud is placed not atop the filter screen, but underneath it in the bulbous glass end. The filter is replaced. A lighter flame is held under the bowl until the bud is emitting a fine stream.

More vapor is produced by vigorously shaking the pipe, and then inhaling as with a normal pipe.

Shake'N Vap™ Review

Tester was wary of a vaporizer that's heat is controlled by fire. Although the simple, clean design resembles a crack pipe, make no mistake; it's a vaporizer designed for herb.

Material is finely ground and put into the large chamber. A screen fits over the top of the bowl and works to keep the material in the pipe when shaking. The herb is heated with a lighter held under the bowl about a half-inch away.

When vapor is seen filling the chamber, take a toke. Now shake the material, swirling it in the bowl and take another toke. Heat and shake, shake and heat. Pull off the screen, tap out the bowl and load it up again. Tester found that practice was the key. The more Tester smoked, the better at it Tester got.

Tester likes the price and portability, though durability is in question. Tester is sometimes clumsy and/or careless. The long slender stem on this vaporizer wouldn't have a long lifespan around this tester. It was shuffled from spot to spot when not in use in an attempt to keep it whole. Tester feared the worst; it wouldn't be the first piece of broken glassware. It survived the testing, performed as advertised, and its ease of use was a pleasant surprise.

The Ubie™
$10
Heat element: flame

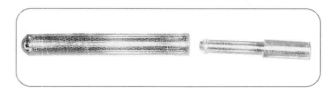

A second pipe-style device, the Ubie™ is designed to be a smokeless glass cigarette. It uses flame to diffuse hot air over the material to produce a vapor. It is the vaporizer's answer to a one-hitter.

The Ubie™ can be held in the mouth while applying flame indirectly to the far end of the pipette. It is kind of like a repeated lighting of a cigarette. The flame is held far enough below the Ubie™ so it does not touch the glass. After applying flame, don't forget which end of the pipe is hot and which is cool. Once the bud is cashed, the cylinder is easily tapped out.

Ubie™ Review

The Ubie™ looks like a glass cigarette and works in a similar way with one huge exception – the flame shouldn't touch the glass. Here's how it works: A small amount of prepared herb is put into the Ubie™. The mouthpiece is replaced and the herb in tapped away from the end and toward the mouthpiece. A lighter is held approximately half an inch under the end farthest from the mouthpiece.

Hot air is forced around the herb while air is being drawn. Tester knows this may sound confusing, and once again, there is a learning curve for perfected use. Hang in there folks; the Ubie™ is a great travel vaporizer that's smaller than most pens. Tester found this unit much more user-friendly than expected. Practicing and following the directions is the key.

The best part is the price. At $10 anyone can afford to try this portable, no-electricity, low-profile, well-thought-out, party-friendly, tiny vaporizer.

RESOURCES

Most companies are discreet enough to send any products in non-descript packaging. If you have any questions about these products, contact the company using the following contact information:

Grinders: _____

Sweetleaf™ Grinders
20 Clematis Road
Toronto, Ontario
Canada M2J 4X2
416-497-9897
416-497-1557 fax
party@sweetleafgrinder.com
www.sweetleafgrinder.com

Featured Vaporizers: _____
BC Vaporizer™
17 East 6th Ave.
Vancouver BC V5T 1J3
604-876-4494
604-876-4847 fax
info@bcvaporizer.com
www.bcvaporizer.com

Eterra Tulip™
Solaria
PO Box 3084
Berkeley, CA 94703
510-595 3779 fax
www.lightwell.net

Vrip Tech™
969-G Edgewater Blvd, # 229
Foster City, CA 94404
info@vriptech.com
www.vriptech.com

PotCooker™
builder@potcooker.com
www.potcooker.com

Vapor Cannon™
www.vapordoc.com

Volcano™
Superjoint Venture
Gyroscoopweg 124
1042 AZ, Amsterdam
The Netherlands
+31 62 752 4244
+31 20 423 1474 fax
www.grasscity.com

Vapir™
Advanced Inhalation
Revolutions Inc.
8950 West Olympic Blvd.
Suite#421
Beverly Hills, California 90211
310-289-3331
310-495-3001 fax
customerservice@air-2.com
www.air-2.com

Cool Vapors™
541-485-6717
danbo@efn.org
www.coolvapors.com

Eagle Bill Shake n' Vap™
Superjoint Venture
Gyroscoopweg 124
1042 AZ, Amsterdam
The Netherlands
+31 6 275 24244
+31 20 423 1474 fax
www.grasscity.com

Ubie™
info@smoke-right.com
www.smoke-right.com

Other Vaporizers: _____

We were unable to review all of the many models currently on the market; however most models now available are similar in design to those described. Our inability to feature every available vaporizer is in no way intended as comment on models that were not included here. In fact, we recommend that individuals interested in vaporization contact these additional vaporizer companies or visit their web sites for further information.

Cheap Vaporizer
Smokeless glass cigarette
(same design as Ubie™) $15
webmaster@cheapvaporizer.com
www.cheapvaporizer.com

De Verdamper BV
Heat-Gun style
Available in 110
and 220 voltage.
300-400 euros for kit
Postbus 251
1700 AG Heerhugowaard
Nederland
+ 31 72 572 5786
+ 31 72 572 5784 fax

Fosheezee™ Vaporizers
Dome chamber type with electric conduction heat element.
$54.99-$99.99
P.O. Box 53509
310-377 Royal Oak Dr.
Victoria, British Columbia
V8X-5K2 Canada
250-389-8911

VapoTron™
Dome chamber type with electric heat element. Different designer bases available. $75
sales@hightides.org
www.hightides.org

Herbal Vaporizer.com™
Handheld dome chamber type
220-volt model, 110-volt
adaptor available
$75
Pure THC
P.O. Box 6641
Halifax Street
Adelaide, 5001
Australia
info@purethc.com
www.herbalvaporizer.com

Inavap™
Compact convection model, $85
JasonSimonson@INAVAP
P.O. Box 1317
Minneapolis,MN 55414
info@inavap.com
www.inavap.com

Vapie™
Compact, conduction unit with
circuit board temperature control
$129.95
Located in Portland, OR
customerservice@vapie.com
www.vapie.com

VaporTech™
Heating console with insertion
bowl and tubing for inhale. $140
VaporTech
PO Box 310206
Miami, FL 33321
888-453-1996 phone and fax
vaportechco@yahoo.com
www.vaportechco.com

Volatizer™
Wand-style model
$199.95-$229.95
Available in U.S. and Canada only.
Chiro-Tec, Inc.
628 Calle Plano
Camarillo, CA 93012
800-485-7305
805-445-9027 fax
chiro-tec@juno.com
www.volatizer.com

Do-It-Yourself Vaporizers:
A number of web sites offer information and explanations. The
PotCooker™ featured in the
chapter is one do-it-yourself
model. Another web site with
information is:
http://nepenthes.lycaeum.org/Dr
ugs/THC/Vaporize/index.html
This information is provided as a
resource. We have not tested the
methods it advocates. Those
interested in building their own
vaporizer will have to make their
own assessment as to the accuracy
of these instructions and assume
their own risk in following them.

3

KIEF

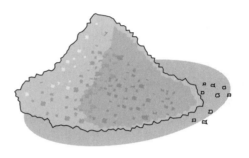

KIEF is an easy process but a controversial word. Alternately spelled as *kif, kief, kef* and *kiff,* it appears in many languages around the world. Kief is a powder that consists of the loose glands shaken free of marijuana buds and plant material. It looks like sand. Some marijuana enthusiasts debate the use of the word *kief,* because this term was originally used in cultures such as Morocco to mean a mixture of grass and tobacco. In Amsterdam and other parts of Europe, kief is sometimes called *pollen* or *polm.* In French and Afrikaans, the word *kief* is also a slang term that means cool or great.

Countries close to the 30th parallel, including Nepal, Afghanistan and Lebanon, have traditionally made kief using a silk scarf stretched tightly over a bowl. The fine weave of the cloth allows the THC glands to pass through,

43

separating them from the vegetative material. Scarves are still used in parts of the world, but plastic silk screening or wire mesh is now often favored. These modern materials are durable, easier to frame, and have standard sizes, which allow for finer sifting.

Kief can be smoked just how it is, but it is often pressed to make hash. It can also be used to produce tinctures or cooking ingredients. This chapter explains various screening techniques to produce kief. Pressing kief is discussed in chapter 5, and other uses appear in their respective chapters.

DEFINING KIEF   ASK ED

Ed:
What is kief?
The Green Wizdad,
Benicia, California

Wizdad:
Kief is composed of the unpressed glands scraped from dried mature flowers and leaves using a screen. Traditionally, they were mixed with tobacco and smoked in hookahs in tea shops throughout Morocco.

In modern grass-growing countries, kief is becoming very popular because it can be gleaned from leaves and trim. It is most typically sifted using a 100 line-per-inch silk or stainless steel mesh.

HOW KIEF SCREENING WORKS

Chapter 1 described the presence of THC-bearing glands on many parts of the marijuana plant. Screening plant material for kief is one of the easiest ways to rescue these glands.

Screening works because glands are consistently within a certain size range. These sizes are often given in microns, which is a metric measurement equal to one millionth of a meter. Glands range between 75-125 microns in size. Maturity, variety and environmental conditions determine gland size. For instance, Moroccan varieties may have glands that are under 80 microns. According to Holland growers, sativa glands are also typically small, while "hash plant" varieties have glands that are often 120 microns or larger. Most sinsemilla, or seedless marijuana, is in the mid-range, between 80-110 microns.

Plant material is shaken over a fine screen, which allows the glands to fall through with only minimal vegetation. Different grades of kief are produced depending on the amount of sifting time, the size of the screen, and the pressure used when sifting. Often the same material is sifted a few times. With each repeated sift, a higher proportion of impurities mixes with the glands, lowering the quality. The color will range from a light tan for the purest kief to a greenish gold, which indicates that vegetative material containing chlorophyll has also filtered through the screen with the glands.

PREPARING TRASH FOR SCREENING

Very little preparation is needed to sieve plant material for kief. In fact, kief making is so quick that small quantities can be done while the trash is being sorted or prepared for another process. It can also be done in large batches. Kief is best made from dried, coarse trash. The stems can be sorted out, but don't have to be. Bud bits can also be sorted out or left in.

The best kief comes from trim and leaf that is dry, but not crisp. Very dry material is brittle, and will crumble into smaller pieces or dust that can pass through the screen. Kief from such material will contain more vegetative matter and won't be as clean. Pressed material or "brick" marijuana does not work as well for kief as loose material does.

GLANDS AND SCREENS: A GUIDE TO MEASUREMENTS

Glands are typically between 75-125 microns in size. The middle of this range, 100 microns, converts as follows:

100 microns = 0.1 millimeter = 0.0039 inches

Screens are chosen with a slightly larger gap than the gland size to ensure that the glands can pass through. Screening material is sized in a few different ways.

Wire mesh screens are sized by either a "mesh" or a "space" measurement. A "space" measure indicates the micron size of the openings between the wires, which should be 100-130 microns for kief sifting.

"Mesh" is a measurement used by wire cloth companies when referring to the strands of wire woven into each square inch of the material. Standard screens for kief making are 100-150 strands per inch. The spaces between the wires for these mesh sizes are roughly 75-125 microns. However, gap size will differ based on how thick the wire is. Wire cloth comes in many types of metals and weaves. The best type to get is "plain" or square wire mesh made of stainless steel.

Silk-screen material is convenient because it is often already framed in wood or aluminum. Silk screen is more flexible than wire mesh. The sizes are given by mesh count, which is the same as mesh for wire cloth. Standard sizes range between 110-195 strands per inch. Between 100-150 is good for making kief. Wire cloth is sturdier and more precise, whereas silk screen is more pliable. Framed silk screen can be found through art supply sources. A few companies that sell wire mesh and silk screen are listed in the resource section at the end of this chapter.

When to Sieve

In the mountains of the Hindu Kush region, hashmakers have traditionally waited for cold, dry weather to sift plant material. The cold weather freezes the dry leaves and trim, making the connection between the bulbous glands and the tiny hair-like cilia brittle and easy to break. Since the glands snap free more easily, it was believed that less vegetative material ended up in the kief. It is true that the brittleness makes the glands break loose easily, but it can also make the trim and leaves more delicate, allowing finely ground plant material to sift through.

Many sources still recommend sifting in very cold weather as a good way to make large quantities of hash in a quick and easy manner. When the material is very cold, the thick oils of the resin will not clog the screening material.

Kief of decent quality can actually be made in all weather conditions. To make kief of the finest caliber, cool temperatures, around 60 degrees F or lower, are best. Low to moderate humidity is okay, and the presence of a little humidity is even welcome if the material is particularly dry.

MANUAL SCREENING

Manual screening is cost effective and no more labor intensive than sifting flour. It is possible to buy ready-made screens or kief boxes from many sources and in many sizes. The screen, usually wire mesh, comes framed and often includes a solid bottom drawer where the kief is collected. See the resources at the end of the chapter for sources on ready-made screens.

Bubble Box – by Fresh Headies

It is also possible to make your own screen. Wire mesh or silk-screen material can be bought from print supply shops or wire cloth sellers. Some resources are listed at the end of the chapter.

If you build your own screen or have a screen without a tray, a piece of glass or mirror will be useful to catch the filtered material. A credit card, business card or other straight edge can be used to gather the filtered material into a pile.

The Screening Process

Place the collection tray under the screen. Start with a handful of trim and leaf. Rub the material softly against the screen. A softer touch will allow only the potent glands to pass through without rubbing free much vegetative matter. This first layer of powder is the cleanest and most potent.

Even the cleanest screened kief will always contain some vegetative matter. Some people pass the material through multiple screens to increase purity. In the first pass, they use a screen that is coarser, under 100 strands

MAKING YOUR OWN SCREEN
Equipment:

- Thick wooden picture frame, or a frame constructed of wood at least 1" x 1"

- Wire cloth cut to fit over the frame and wrap around to the underside

- 3/8-inch wire tacks or staplegun

Cut the wire cloth to fit over the frame, adding enough length to wrap around the side. (For instance, if the wood frame is 6 inches x 6 inches, cut the wire cloth at 8 inches x 8 inches, which leaves an extra inch on each side.)

Pull screen taut and tack or staple it to the side or bottom of the frame.

per inch. This first screening cleans out the bulk of the vegetative matter. The sifted material is then placed atop a finer screen and shaken or tapped lightly. Since the vegetative material is only tapped through the second screen, not pushed, the multi-screening method yields cleaner results.

Often, kief makers will sift the same material several times. The first sift is usually light and short in duration —from a minute to 15 minutes, depending on the amount of material and size of the screen. The biggest, most mature glands are the first to break free and sift through. This is the highest quality kief, but the yield is fairly low.

The material can be sifted again for longer and with slightly more pressure. The less mature glands now fall, but so do some of the hair-like stems to which they were attached. Plant material that has crumbled into dust is also small enough to pass through the screen. The second sift will produce a larger quantity of kief that is still potent, but contains more vegetative material and isn't as pure as the first screening. The color will likely reveal this, being slightly darker or possibly greener.

In manual screening, a soft touch is as important as the environmental conditions for good results. Experimentation will help the novice figure out how much pressure to apply for a good yield without too much vegetative matter.

SPACE CASE® GRINDER/POLLEN COLLECTOR

This slick, hockey-puck-looking stash case is a combination grinder/storage/gland collection unit. Made from tooled aluminum, the grinder/pollen collector comes in two sizes and costs between $45-$65.

The grinder mechanism at the top chops material, which collects in a chamber below it. Seeds slip easily from the grinder into the collection chamber making them easy to remove. Simply open the collection chamber to access the smoke-ready material. But that's not all. A fine screen filter serves as the bottom of the grinder's chamber. A second reservoir below the grinder chamber catches kief. This simple innovation allows you to salvage valuable glands that are often lost in preparation. Use the collected kief every time you grind, or be patient and let it build up for that special bowl. This material could also be collected and saved, pressed into hash or used in cooking.

For information on purchasing this product, see the resource section at the end of the chapter.

Manual kief screening is good for making small amounts at any one time, and is cheap and easy to do. To process larger amounts of plant material or produce a cleaner product with less elbow grease, upgrading to a drum machine is a worthwhile investment.

MACHINE SCREENING

If you have a lot of leaf and trim that you'd like to screen for kief, manual screening can be tiresome. Luckily, some other folks have already discovered this and come up with inventions that take the labor out of kief making.

Drum machines like Tumble Now® and The Pollinator® are simple devices that gather a higher percentage of glands from the plant material than flat screening can.

The Pollinator®

The Pollinator® is the original drum machine developed by Mila Jansen in the Netherlands. Mila is a natural innovator. A hash aficionado who was born in the Netherlands and lived for years in the Hindu Kush region, Mila has spent her fair share of time manually screening leaf and trim to make kief.

Many years ago, cold weather had set into the mountains of Northern India. Since it is believed that the trichomes snap more cleanly from the plant when the material is frozen, cold weather meant it was time to screen. She and friends spent several chilly days manually screening loads of trim for powder. The repetitive nature of screening was tedious and tiring.

One evening after a long day of screening, Mila returned home and in the late hours, she stood, tired from the day's work, waiting for the laundry to finish. Suddenly

her attention shifted to the clothes dryer. She was struck with the brilliant simplicity of her idea. The dryer was essentially doing what she'd been doing all day! Soon thereafter, she invented the Pollinator®.

Mila worked out a model for personal use, but it would be a few years before it occurred to her that this machine might be marketable.

The Pollinator® is available in a few sizes depending on one's needs. Resembling a clothes dryer, it is electrically powered. Trash is placed inside it and the machine is turned on. The material is softly tossed against a fine screen, around 130 strands per inch. The amount of time it is allowed to turn determines the quality of the kief that is collected.

This machine makes creating kief or hash ridiculously simple. It can be used over and over. The same material can be reprocessed according to the collector's wishes. A+ hash can be collected by briefly pollinating the material and removing the powder. Then the same material can be screened again. Information for contacting the Pollinator Company appears in the resource section at the end of the chapter. Presses and water hash (Ice-o-lator®) equipment are also available through the Pollinator Company.

A PRESSING ISSUE: KIEF AND HASH

Once kief is made, it can be used in a number of ways. The glands are delicious smoked fresh and loose. However, some traditionalists insist that they be pressed into hash. Chapter 5 explains how to make hash from kief, which is one of the cheapest and easiest ways to make hash at home. Hash made from screened kief, especially using the first-grade kief, should be quite good.

Kief can also be processed into tinctures (chapter 6) or capsules (chapter 7). It can also work well for cooking (chapter 8) because it lacks the strong green flavor that some people find unpleasant in cannabis foods.

Screening for kief, whether manually or with the help of a machine, is a fabulous way to recycle plant material that was destined for the garbage can. It is less labor intensive, less expensive, and less time consuming for the yield than most other processes.

RESOURCES

Ready-Made Screens: ——————————————————————————

**Fresh Headies Bubble Box®
and Screen Kit**
www.freshheadies.com
1-866-635-8464

Whiskey Falls Kief Boxes
2281 South G St.
Fresno, CA 93721
877-565-9084
sales@whiskeyfalls.com
www.whiskeyfalls.com

Wonder Wood Box
info@wonderwoodbox.com
www.wonderwoodbox.com

Treetop Glass Kief Boxes
P.O. BOX 26301
Eugene, OR 97402
877-655-3932
541-688-3932
treetop@treetopglass.com
www.treetopglass.com

Superpiece.com Box
www.superpiece.com

Screen Material: ────────────────────────

Wire Mesh

Howard Wire Cloth Co.
Sells internationally;
no minimum order.
28976 Hopkins St.
Hayward CA 94545
800-969-3559
510-786-4167 fax
sales@howardwire.com
www.howardwire.com

Silk Screen

Dick Blick Art Materials
P.O. Box 1267
Galesburg, IL 61402
800-828-4548
309-343-6181 international
info@dickblick.com
www.dickblick.com

F.P. Smith
F.P. Smith sells internationally:
$50 minimum order, wire
mesh sells for approx $10/
square foot.
11700 West Grand Avenue
Northlake, Illinois 60164
800-323-6842
800-310-8999 fax
www.fpsmith.com

Fault Line Graphics
1487 Callens Rd.
Ventura, CA 93003
888-374-3444
info@faultlinegraphics.com
www.faultlinegraphics.com

Drum Machines: ────────────────────────

The Pollinator®
Pollinator Company
Nieuwe Herengracht 25
1011 RL, Amsterdam Holland
+31 20 470-8889
+31 20 471-5242 fax
info@pollinator.nl
www.pollinator.nl

Tumble Now® Machine
Fresh Headies
www.freshheadies.com
1-866-635-8464

4

WATER HASH

OVER the last decade, water hash has fast become a favorite in Europe and Canada. Its name comes from the efficient water process that is used to collect glands from the trim, leaf and bud bits. Water hash is actually a loose, kief-type product that can be smoked as is, or pressed into traditional hashish form. Either way, many people are quickly converted once they've experienced this pure and potent product.

Water hash can be made in small or large quantities. Ready-made systems can be purchased to simplify the process. These systems have increased the precision and efficiency of the water hash process, and contributed to its surge in popularity. It is also possible to make water hash using home-gathered equipment.

HOW WATER HASH WORKS

The water method uses a combination of water, ice and agitation to separate glands from the plant material. Ice, water and plant material are placed in a bucket that has been lined with bags. These filtration bags are similar to the screens used in making kief. They filter the glands by micron size, separating the trash from the hash. A micron is one-millionth of a meter, or .001 millimeters (see Glands & Screens for more info, p. 46). The material is stirred to knock the trichomes free. Plant material is trapped and floats in the top bag, while the glands, which are heavy enough to sink, are collected in the lower bag.

Some ready-made systems use multiple bags that sort the glands into grades. Unlike kief making, the material is separated in one step rather than through repeated sieving. The same material can still be processed more than once to ensure that all the available THC has been salvaged.

The ice serves a dual purpose. It acts as an agitator against which the material is scuffed. It also makes the material very cold, causing the connection between the glands and the plant material to become brittle. After the material is agitated in ice water, it is allowed to settle, and then the bags are separated, and so are the glands. After the water hash dries, it is ready to smoke.

Water hash varies in color, much like kief. The finest grade is typically a light tan, while the coarser second-tier material is slightly darker and may be a little green from plant material contamination. Many people are surprised by how the hash turns to liquid, melts and bubbles when it is smoked.

The quality of water hash, especially from the finest grade material, is impressive. Of course, as with the other

Ed:

I saw some products advertised to make water hash, and I was thinking about getting one.

Do these products really work? Is one better than another? Do I really need one of these to make hash or can I do it without one? Is there a difference between water hash and regular hash?

Thanks,

Hash Rookie,

Ottawa, Ontario Canada

Rookie:

Hash is made by sifting dried plant matter for glands using silk screen or stainless steel mesh. The resulting powder is pressed. Water hash also uses a screening process. Glands are removed from the plant using filters, but this is done while the grass is in a combination of ice and water.

The main difference is in the filtration method. Water hash methods usually use several screens, assuring a more homogeneous product. The resulting water hash can be extremely high in quality.

Both methods work and are worth the effort. For water hash, the ready-made bag systems are a great way to go. These bags can be used over and over again. The two most popular models, the Ice-o-lator® and Bubble Bags®, are both well-made systems that should give consistent results and withstand the test of time.

It is also possible to make water hash without a bag system. One such method agitates the material in ice and water. The bulk of the plant material floats and is removed with a colander. The material that sank to the bottom of the container is mostly glands. It looks grayish or tan in the water. It is rinsed out of the container and captured in a coffee filter. This method contains a small amount of vegetative material, so it won't be as pure.

processes in the book, the high produced from water hash depends upon the quality of the plants being used. Processing plant material with water yields hash that has been washed free of contaminants: green plant matter, mold, fungi, and chemicals.

It is possible to extract 1/4 ounce-1 ounce of hash from every 8 ounces of plant material. The yield depends in part on the number of glands present on the material. Buds and A+ trim will have a higher concentration of THC trichomes, so the yields will be higher.

The entire process takes three to six hours to complete. The bag method is kind of like doing the laundry; it does not require constant attention, but is something that you keep coming back to at regular intervals. This chapter covers the main methods for making water hash. The next chapter will explain how to press it.

WATER HASH BASICS

Any gland-bearing plant material can be used to make water hash, including leaf, trim, buds, shake, or a combination. The material works best when it has been dried first, although it is also possible to use fresh plant material.

More importantly, the process works best when the material is cold. In humid areas, it is a good idea to store dried material in the freezer to avoid deterioration or molds. When using material that has not been stored in this way, place the material in the freezer until it gets cold.

Since glands reside on the surfaces of the plant, the material does not need to be ground to make water hash. Small cuttings or coarsely chopped material is most convenient. Remove any big twigs or stems, as they could tear the bags.

Whether using a ready-made bag system or materials from your kitchen, the basic principles of making water hash are the same. Aside from the caliber of the plant material, the quality of the filter determines the purity of the results.

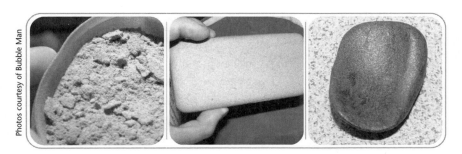

Photos courtesy of Bubble Man

READY-MADE BAGS

Several ready-made bag systems are on the market, but two have become the most popular systems for making water hash. These are the Ice-o-lator® from Mila at the Pollinator Company, and Bubble Bags® from Fresh Headies in Canada.

Both systems provide high-quality bags that are durable, and easy to clean and use. The bags are color-coded for convenience. Bubble Bags® may be more commonly known in North America because the company is based in Canada, while the Ice-o-lator® system hails from Amsterdam and is probably more widely known in Europe, but both products are available internationally.

The Ice-o-lator®

Mila Jansen's first invention was the Pollinator®, which is discussed in chapter 3. Her interest in improving hash-making methods also lead her to develop the ready-made water extraction system called the Ice-o-lator®.

59

According to Mila, experiments with a water process did not yield much, literally, until a product called the Extractor was released in 1997. This machine was sold from the U.S. and manufactured in Yugoslavia. After

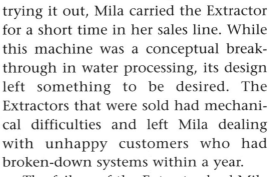
The Ice-o-lator®

trying it out, Mila carried the Extractor for a short time in her sales line. While this machine was a conceptual breakthrough in water processing, its design left something to be desired. The Extractors that were sold had mechanical difficulties and left Mila dealing with unhappy customers who had broken-down systems within a year.

The failure of the Extractor lead Mila to experiment with her own design, using the principles by which the Extractor worked. She created a simpler, manual system that is called the Ice-o-lator®. This bag system first became available in 1998. It has since been refined and expanded to include three standard sizes that can process 200-1200 grams of material at a time, plus a travel Ice-o-lator®, and a large system that can be used in the washing machine.

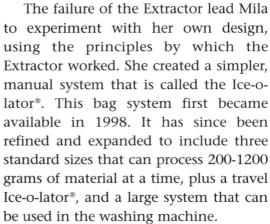

The Ice-o-lator® consists of two bags, which line a sealable bucket of the appropriate size. Ice and water are added and then the dried material is placed in the bucket. A standard kitchen mixer affixed through the bucket's lid agitates the material. The top bag holds all of the vegetative matter. Glands filter through the silk screen of the first bag and collect in the finer screen of the second bag. The remaining water in the bucket will have particulate vegetative matter, including some nutrients that make it good for watering house-plants or vegetable gardens.

Prices for Ice-o-lator® systems range between 80 and 180 euros—roughly equivalent to the same amount in dollars at this time. They can be shipped anywhere in the world. Further information on this product is available in the resource section at the end of this chapter.

Bubble Bags®

Bubble Bags®

Bubble Bags® are the design of Fresh Headies in Canada. Bubble Man, the head hashmaster of Fresh Headies, has traveled extensively, spreading the good word on water hash. He can also be found moderating in online forums on this topic.

Bubble Bags® Bubble Bags are available in one-gallon, five-gallon and twenty-gallon sizes. All sizes are available as either a four-bag or an eight-bag system. Bubble Bags range in price from $95 for a one-gallon system to $650 for the twenty-gallon, eight-bag system.

Eight-bag systems separate the hash into finer categories. The size difference between just-ripe THC glands and overly mature or premature ones allows them to be separated into grades.

Bubble Bags® work in a similar but slightly modified way from the Ice-o-lator® system. First, the coarse filter bag is secured in a bucket and the water, ice and plant material are added. The material is agitated using a kitchen mixer or a drill with a paint-mixing attachment. After the material settles, the starter bag is pulled out and squeezed. The bulk of the plant material now held in this bag is set aside. This material can be processed again.

The empty bucket is lined with the additional bags—either two or five, depending on the system. The finest bag goes in first, so it will be on the bottom. The green water is poured into the second bucket, which is lined with the filtering bags. These bags are pulled out one by one, and the material in the bottom of each one is collected and allowed to dry. The water can be tossed out or used for watering plants.

Homemade Bags

It is possible to make your own bags, or to make a smaller amount of water hash without using bags at all. To make bags, acquire silk screen in the appropriate mesh size. Standard silk-screen material is available in several size increments between the desired 100-150 strands per inch.

Check with the local art-supply store, or see the resource section at the end of the chapter for silk screen suppliers. The material must be attached to a tightly woven, water-resistant material (nylon works well) so that the silk-screen forms the bottom of the bag. Multiple bags can be made with different screening levels in the 50-150 micron range for separating the water hash by quality.

The finest screen will produce the purest hash. If

multiple bags are made, they should be designed to fit inside one another, with the finest mesh bag being the largest and the coarsest mesh being the smallest. A separate bag made for coarse filtering (200-250 micron-sized gaps) is also good for separating out the bulk of the vegetation in the first phase. This bag should line the bucket size that will be used. It does not get layered with the other bags, so it should be as large as the bucket allows.

See the small-scale Coffee Filter and Jar methods for processing water hash without bags.

THE BUCKET METHOD

The essentials of the water hash method are the same, whether using a ready-made system, or working from your own homemade bags.

EQUIPMENT

- Ice
- Cold water
- Hydrogen peroxide
- 2 buckets with at least one lid
- Dried trim/bud/leaf material
- Handheld mixer or drill with paint-mixing attachment
- Ready-made bag system or homemade bags
- Long rubber gloves
- Large towel
- Roll of paper towels
- Spoon or plastic card

Method

First, the buckets and equipment should be cleaned and sterilized. Mix 10 ounces (1-1/4 cups) of 3% hydrogen peroxide per quart of water to make a rinse.

If you are using a bag in the first round, place this bag in the bucket. Add equal amounts of ice and water until the bucket is 2/3 full. Add the prepared plant material. Wearing the long rubber gloves, use your hands to submerse it evenly in the ice water. Up to 3-1/2 ounces (100 g) of plant material can be used in a 5-gallon bucket.

If a kitchen mixer is being used, holes are punched in a bucket lid to accommodate the mixing attachments. This keeps the material from sloshing out while it is being agitated. It also allows the mixer to run hands-free.

Using the tool of choice (kitchen mixer or drill with paint-mixing attachment), agitate the material for 15 minutes, and then allow the mixture to settle. If using a ready-made system, the speed recommended in the instructions should be used. As a general rule of thumb, lower speeds work well when mixing amounts under five gallons. Medium to high speeds are better when using a system that is 5 gallons or larger. After mixing, the material will become frothy. You may want to rearrange the material before recommencing.

Blend the material one to four times for 15 minutes at a time. Mixing the material more times produces higher yields, but also results in more particulate vegetative matter. Longer times may give less pure results, especially if multiple bags aren't separating the hash into grades. When using a single collection mechanism, a shorter time can be used on the first round. After this hash is collected, the plant material can be reprocessed using a longer mixing time. Multiple bags allow the material to be processed all at once without sacrificing a high-grade collection.

Once the last mixing round is completed, let the mixture sit for at least 30 minutes. This allows the glands time to sink into the collection filters. If all of the ice has melted,

WATER HASH TIPS

- Using cold, dried material works best. If the material was not stored in the freezer, it should be placed in the freezer until it is cold. If you have too much material to place it in the freezer, don't worry; just make sure you have extra ice. Place a few inches of water in the bucket, add the plant material, and fill the remainder of the bucket with ice. Allow the mixture to sit and cool for 30 minutes before beginning.

- It is better to use a standard two-beater mixer or drill with a paint-mixing attachment. The mini or handheld, one-piece mixers do not have the same agitating power. They also work by pulling material up to the spinning blade. Stringy pieces of plant material could easily clog this type of machine.

- Don't get impatient in the final steps! Dry the material thoroughly at the end of the process. If water hash is stored before it is dried, it will be inclined to mold, ruining your efforts.

- Water left over at the end of the process contains water-soluble nutrients that were present in the plant material. It's great for watering other plants.

more can be added. In cold weather, the bucket can be set outside to keep the mixture cold.

Once the material has settled, it is time to separate out the glands. If the agitation has been done inside a bag, this bag should be pulled out, removing the bulk of the plant material. The bucket now contains green water with silt in the bottom. This silt is the water hash and a small amount of particulate vegetative matter.

Line the second bucket with the collection bag or bags. The finest mesh bag goes on the bottom, so it is added to the bucket first. The coarsest bag is the last bag added, so it is the top layer. The first bag has separated out everything over the 200-250 micron size, depending on its mesh size. Now the successive layers of the bag will do the grading for you.

Pour the water into the bucket that is lined with the filter bags. Slowly lift out each bag, allowing time for the water to drain. Be patient. If the entire bottom of the bag seems to be clogged, it may be necessary reach in and gently push some material to the side. Avoid stirring up the material if possible.

After each bag is removed, lay it on the towel and pat off excess water. More water can be removed by wrapping it with paper towels and squeezing it. The inside of each bag contains some tan to brown silt-like material. Carefully arrange the bag so that the material is accessible. Blot the material off with a paper towel. Remove it from the bag using a credit card or a spoon. If multiple bags were used, keep the grades separated.

Place the material in a flat-bottomed bowl, or on a plate or other surface where it can be left to dry. It is best to place the material in a cool, dark place where it will get some airflow, but won't blow away once dry. Material is fairly dry after 12 hours, but a full week allows it to dry and cure fully. Even if some material is used sooner, allow the moisture to evaporate from the remaining material so it is not susceptible to mold.

THE COFFEE FILTER METHOD

This method works well for small-scale water hash production and uses common kitchen equipment. The plant material should be chopped to a coarsely ground consistency. Cone-type coffeemakers look like a pointier version of a standard coffeemaker basket. They are very cheap (under $5) and are available at kitchenware stores, some gourmet coffee shops, grocery stores or on the web. The #4 size or larger is recommended. Both the re-usable and disposable filters for these cones should be available at the same places where the cone was purchased.

This method yields nice hash, but the process is not controlled by precise micron-sized filters. There is also no final filtration of small vegetative matter, so the product is not as pure as the hash made in a bag system. Still, the water hash produced using this method equals the quality of dry-screened kief.

EQUIPMENT

- Ice
- Cold water
- Dried plant material (coarsely ground)
- Blender
- Mixing bowl
- Colander or wire mesh strainer
- Cone-type single cup coffee maker
- Re-usable metal cone coffee filter, or silk screening

- Coffee filters
- 2-3 large glass jars with tight-sealing lids
- Dish towel
- Paper towels
- Scraping tool (spoon, credit card or business card)

Method

Place enough plant material in the blender to fill it halfway. Add ice and cold water in equal amounts until the blender is full. Turn the blender on at full speed for 45 seconds to 1 minute. Let the mixture settle. This can be repeated three or four times. The more times the blender is run, the higher the yield; however, more vegetative material will also become particulate and lower the purity of the results.

Pour the mixture from the blender through a colander or strainer into a mixing bowl. Bowls designed to pour, such as a pancake batter bowl or an 8-cup measuring cup work best. This step separates out the bulk of the plant material.

Now pour this water through the re-usable coffee filter into the glass jars, until they are about 2/3 full. Quart-sized sealable glass canning jars work well. Material will collect in the coffee filter. This is the smaller vegetative matter. The glands are too small to stay in the re-usable coffee filter and have passed with the water into the glass jars. Pour another cup or two of water through the filter into the glass jars to wash out any remaining glands.

Seal the jars and place them in the fridge for at least 30 minutes. The glands settle and form silt at the bottom of the jar. Tapping the jar lightly a few times on a tabletop may help settle some material that persistently floats.

Without stirring up the material that has collected in the bottom of the jars, remove them from the refrigerator, and pour off the top 1/2-2/3 of the water. The object is to retain the glands that are gathered in the bottom, while removing as much water content as possible.

Set up the cone on top of a suitable container. Drain the remaining water and silt through the coffee cone that is lined with a disposable paper coffee filter. As the material collects, the water will filter through more slowly. Allow the water to completely drain.

Carefully remove the paper coffee filter from the cone. Allow it to flatten with the material trapped inside. Pat the filter with a towel.

FOR MORE THAN ONE BLENDER BATCH:

To shorten the process when blending more than one batch, follow the steps for the first blender batch up to the point where 1/2-2/3 of the water content is removed. At this point, complete a second blender batch. When you reach the point where the filtered material is poured into the jars, add it to the top of the already settled material. Ice can also be added to the jars to keep the material cold. Place the full jars back in the fridge and allow to settle for another 30 minutes. Pour the water off the top again. This can be repeated as many times as desired before proceeding to the final filtering step.

Material can be dried before it is collected from the coffee filter or after. Drying it inside the coffee filter may take a little longer, but the hash is protected from blowing away and is easier to remove from the paper when both are no longer wet. To dry in the coffee filter, place the filter atop a layer of paper towels. Once dried, it can be split along a seam.

Collect the material using a spoon or plastic or paper card. It is desirable to allow the material to fully dry before pressing or storing, which takes 12 hours to a few days, depending on the environmental conditions and the amount being dried.

Photos: C.P.O.

Variations on the Coffee Filter Method

- Thoroughly cleaned glass liter bottles or plastic 2-liter bottles can be recycled for this process, replacing the glass jars. Make sure to keep the lids! Rinse the recycled bottles with a hydrogen peroxide solution (10 ounces of 3% hydrogen peroxide per 1 quart of water) to sterilize them first. A funnel will be needed to transfer the material from the blender to the bottle.

- When it comes time to drain the top $1/2$ - $2/3$ of the water from the container, try siphoning instead of pouring it off for more control and less turbulence. Insert clean, sterilized flexible tubing, such as aquarium tubing, into the jar. Place the other end of the tubing into a sink or other drainage area. Take advantage of gravity by placing the jar higher than the draining end.

- Heating mats can be used to speed up the drying process. Place the mat under a towel and put the drying water hash on top of it. Propagation mats used to sprout seedlings maintain a 74 degree F temperature. Waterproof heating pads set on warm work well too. Food dehydrators set on low are also an effective way to speed up the drying time.

THE JAR SHAKER METHOD

The simplest method for making water hash is using a homemade shaker. This method is the easiest in terms of time and equipment, but it also produces the least amount of hash and won't be as pure as methods using micron-gauged filtering bags. Manual agitation is more labor intensive, but it requires no electricity and can be accomplished anywhere that the materials can be gathered.

EQUIPMENT

- Up to an ounce of marijuana trim, bud bits, or shake
- Water
- Ice
- Sealable glass jar
- Colander or wire mesh strainer
- Slotted spoon or tea strainer
- Coffee cone (#4)
- Paper coffee filters
- Dish towel
- Paper towels

Method

Reduce the marijuana material to a coarse powder, similar to dried cooking herbs like oregano or basil. This can be accomplished by snipping the material, or rubbing it against a wire mesh strainer.

Place the material in the jar, up to 1/4 full. A pint- or quart-sized canning jar works. Add equal amounts of ice and very cold water until the jar is almost full. Leave about an inch of space at the top of the jar, then seal it and shake for 5-10 minutes at a time. Friends can take turns shaking it. The marijuana should disperse in the water. Continue to shake until the plant material is evenly distributed.

Set the jar in the refrigerator and allow it to settle for 30 minutes or longer. Most of the ice will melt in this time.

Open the jar and remove the floating plant material with a tea strainer or slotted spoon. The plant material can be saved and reprocessed. Manual shaking may not remove all trichomes on the first round.

Once the plant material has been removed, allow the silt to resettle at the bottom of the jar for 15-20 minutes.

Drain off 1/2-2/3 of the water slowly, with an eye to saving all of the silt-like material in the bottom of the jar, which is the water hash.

Set up the cone lined with a paper coffee filter. Pour the remaining contents of the shaker jar through the cone. As the water hash collects in the bottom of the filter, the water will drain more slowly. Allow all of the water to drain from the filter. Then remove the filter from the cone, allowing it to flatten with the wet hash inside. Set it on a dish towel and carefully remove as much water as possible by pressing with the towel or paper towels.

Split the coffee filter along the seam and open it like a butterfly. Collect the material inside using a spoon or plastic card to scrape it loose from the paper. The material is easier to separate from the coffee filter when it is either dry or only slightly damp.

The material can dry either before or after it is removed from the filter. Even if some of the material is collected for use before the drying completes, the water hash should be allowed to air dry over a day or two to reduce the chance of mold. After the hash is dry, it can be used, stored or pressed into hash.

PRESSING AND STORAGE

Some people find the aroma and flavor of water hash unusually mild. Water filters out some of the water-soluble chlorophyll and other pigments, as well as some of the terpenes, which give marijuana its taste and scent. The milder qualities of water hash are not an indication of its potency. If a stronger aroma or flavor is desired, Bubble Man recommends pressing some dry-sifted kief with the bubble hash.

When smoked fresh, high-purity water hash will bubble and melt, hence the nickname, "bubble hash." Because of how it reacts when burned, water hash may need to be pressed lightly in order to smoke through a standard pipe. People often press the material in their hands to form balls or triangles. A more thorough press to form a true hashish piece is explained in the next chapter.

Water hash stores best in loose form. Keep it in a sealed container away from light and heat until ready for use.

RESOURCES

Ready-Made Bags:

The Ice-o-lator®
Pollinator Company
Nieuwe Herengracht 25
1011 RL, Amsterdam
Holland
+31-20 470-8889
+31 20 471-5242
info@pollinator.nl
www.pollinator.nl

Bubble Bags®
Fresh Headies
Vancouver, BC, Canada
www.freshheadies.com
1-866-635-8464

Silk Screen:

Fault Line Graphics
1487 Callens Rd.
Ventura, CA 93003
888-374-3444
info@faultlinegraphics.com
www.faultlinegraphics.com

Dick Blick Art Materials
P.O. Box 1267
Galesburg, IL 61402
800-828-4548
309-343-6181 international
info@dickblick.com
www.dickblick.com

5

HASHISH
SIMPLIFIED

HASHISH is a collection of marijuana's resinous glands that have been compressed into balls, cakes or slabs. The origins of hashish date back millennia and are believed to have begun in Asia, near the Hindu Kush region. Hashmaking has a long tradition in many countries near the 30th latitude, including India, Nepal, Afghanistan, Pakistan and Lebanon.

Making hashish is a two-step process. In step one, the glands are collected. All collection methods yield a consumable product, but it is not yet hashish. Hashish involves a second step: compressing the collected material into bricks or balls.

Sifting for kief is the primary low-tech way to collect glands for hash. Water hash can be pressed using the same methods. Another method of collection—hand rubbing—

dates back to ancient times and while low in yield, can produce quality hash. Hand-rubbed hash is collected fresh from the plant, and the resin is still sticky, so the method of pressing involves a slightly different process.

WHAT IS HASHISH?   **ASK ED**

Ed:
What exactly is hash?
Shales,
Oakland, California

Shales:
Hashish, or hash, is a conglomeration of crushed and heated glands or trichomes. Using gentle heat and pressure the gland heads' membranes break, releasing the viscous liquid. The pressure forces out the air leaving the pure mass of crushed glands.

Hash can be made as easily as placing some kief in cellophane, wrapping it carefully, and then placing it inside the heel of your shoe. Walk and stand on it for fifteen to thirty minutes, and unwrap the newly pressed hash. A friend showed me how he makes it using a thin cotton cloth to wrap the kief. Then he presses it using a dry iron. Commercially, hash is made using high-power presses. The most sophisticated of these units heats the material in addition to applying pressure.

Pressing hash involves a combination of force and mild heat to condense the glands into a solid mass. The shape and size of hash can vary depending on the pressing method that is used. When hand pressed, it is often ball-shaped. Flat-pressed hash can look like thin shale rock, with hardened shelf-like layers that chip along the creases. Mechanically pressed hash is usually a neat cake, like a bar of soap. Hashish also ranges in color and pliability. The variety of marijuana used, the pressing method, and the purity of the hash may all influence its color, which ranges from light yellow-tan to charcoal black.

Aficionados often describe the high that hash produces as more complex than that of unpressed material. In the region of traditional hashmaking, kief is typically aged, sometimes for a year or more, before it is pressed. Most modern or home hashmakers do not want to wait that long.

It is better to store material in its unpressed form. Once pressed, hash stored in the freezer suffers little from aging, but it is a more fragile substance than kief or unpressed water hash. The material is best pressed when it will be used shortly afterward.

Good quality hash is solid at room temperature. It can be supple, bending easily, or dense and brittle. Differences in color and density result from harvesting method, pressing technique, the presence of impurities, storage method and aging. Hashish darkens from exposure to light, oxygen and heat. Regardless of its texture, high-quality hash should soften with the simple warmth of your hands.

COLLECTING FOR HASH

Preparing Kief or Water Hash for Hashmaking

Kief and water hash methods of collection are covered thoroughly in chapters 3 and 4. While these two processes have different advantages, each yields dry loose material that can be pressed to make hash.

Before attempting to press kief or water hash, the material should be completely dry. Just before pressing, the material can be put through a last drying phase to ensure that all moisture has been eliminated. Place the kief or water hash in a food dehydrator set on the lowest setting, or microwave the material on low to remove the last vestiges of water. These precautions against moisture will improve the life span of any hash that is to be stored, guarding it against mold or spoiling due to trapped moisture.

Collecting by Hand: Rubbing for Hash

There are many tales about collecting hash from fresh plants. Hand rubbing for hash has been a common gathering method for centuries in some parts of Asia, and it is still a primary way of collecting for hash in some parts of the world.

Because it requires no equipment, hand rubbing is a novel and spontaneous way to collect for hash, but this method also has several down sides.

First, the effort required to produce a substantial yield is greater than the other methods. It can be messy and labor intensive. Second, hash collected this way is subject to more contaminants from plant debris and hands, and contains more water, making it more likely to spoil. Hand

HASH FACTS

The color and consistency of hash varies considerably. However, it softens and crumbles from very mild heat, even the simple body warmth created by holding it in your hands.

The quality and potency of hash is dependent on several factors. Chief among them is the quality of the plant material from which it was made. Other factors may be the amount of vegetative material, moisture content and age.

Moisture will cause hash to mold. Mold may be indicated by a musty smell. It can also be visible as white streaks within the hash. Moldy hash should never be ingested, as it can make you sick.

Hash burns slow with a fragrance that is incense-like. The flavor of the smoke is often peppery or slightly spicy. It can have floral undertones. When burned, it gives off smoke that is thick white, sometimes with a bluish tint. The resulting ash will be white.

rubbing requires access to mature plants rather than dried trim and leaf, so unlike the other methods, it is only capable of being made at certain times in the growing cycle and cannot be made from trash that has been collected and stored. Removing the collected resin from the hands can be an involved task.

Having pointed out these shortcomings, hand rubbing can be used when the goal is a small amount of quality hash that will be used shortly after it is collected. Especially when the leaves and trim aren't going to be saved, hand rubbing is a good way to salvage some of the THC before or during harvest and manicuring. The total amount collected is likely to be less than an ounce an hour.

The amount of material collected through hand rubbing is dependent on timing and good technique. It is best to collect for hash when the plants' stigmas have started to turn amber as they reach full maturity, but before the leafy material has become brown or dry. The more dead or dry the plant material, the more plant debris will be mixed in with the hash. If the plants are mature and have some dead or dried material, removing these leaves before collection will increase the quality of the hash. Collection should not be done when the plants are wet from watering, as this will increase the water content.

Hand Rubbing Technique

Before starting collection, coat your hands with a little cooking oil, and then pat it off with a towel. The thin oil layer makes the palms a little sticky. This helps not only to attract the first glands, but also makes removing the resin from the hands easier when that time comes.

Rub the plants very lightly, starting at the top of the plant and working down. Remember that the glands are just tiny globules on the ends of the hairs that stick up from buds and leaves. Think of touching a person so that you were brushing the fine hairs while only barely touching the skin. The same technique is used to rub the plants for resin. Glands are only present on the top sides of the leaves, which is why the plant is rubbed from the top down. Within a few minutes of rubbing, the hands will begin to collect the sticky, tar-like resin, and the air will be filled with the plant's heady aroma. High quality resin will create a clear sticky gloss on the palms, darkening to amber as the resin builds up.

Only resin should be collecting on the hands. This is a clear indicator that you have chosen the right time to collect. If lots of specks of plant material are being picked up, or fluid from plant branches is present, the plants may not be mature enough for collection, or you may be rubbing too vigorously. It is nearly impossible to avoid attracting some errant leaf bits and particles onto your sticky hands. Larger plant debris can be brushed off fairly easily without losing any of the collected resin.

Removing the Resin

The collected material is scraped off the hands periodically. Another person can do this, or the collector can do it himself. A blunt-edged scraper can be used to remove resin from the palms. If more resin is going to be collected, leave a little residue on the hands. Another way to remove collected resin from the hands is to rub the hands back and forth against each other, as if trying to warm them up. Take care not to pull the hands apart quickly if they are sticky with resin, as this can raise blisters.

Using water to remove resin from the hands is counterproductive, since the goal is to remove as much water from the hash as possible. Instead of aiding in the removal of the resin, water greatly increases the chances of contamination and spoilage.

Hand-rubbed resin is often pressed by hand. When the material is scraped or rubbed off of the hands, it is kneaded and rolled between the hands until it forms a ball. It is often worked in the hand by rolling it with one palm against the surface of the other palm. It should be worked for several minutes to try to warm it and squeeze out any residual moisture.

Hash made from freshly collected resin can be pressed further, using the methods on the pages that follow, or it can be considered complete after it has been worked into a ball. It is better to use this hash soon after it is made rather than storing it. Because of the fresh resins, vegetative content and presence of water from the live plant material, hand-rubbed hash is more vulnerable to spoilage. If stored, the best place for it is in an opaque container that is not made of plastics or rubber, placed in the freezer.

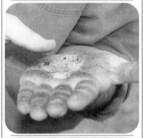

If hash shows signs of molding, such as a mossy smell, or the appearance of grainy white lines along or within the hash, it is ruined and should not be used. These bacteria and molds are no good for you.

PRESSING HASHISH

Pressing transforms the collected material both chemically and physically. The glands are warmed and some are broken, releasing the sticky oils that contain the psychoactive cannabinoids, as well as the terpenes—the source of marijuana's smell and taste.

Terpenes lend fragrance to the hash. Smells and flavors characteristic to hashish range from spicy or peppery to floral in quality. Terpenes are also volatile and contribute to the lung expansiveness, i.e., cough factor, as well as the taste. Aged kief is both milder in smell and flavor, and less cough inducing, because some of the terpenes—not the THC—have dissipated.

Releasing and warming cannabinoids exposes them to air. This has the beneficial effect of potentiating the THC through decarboxylation (see box, next page). Continued exposure to light, air, heat and moisture leads to THC deterioration.

Material can be pressed into hash manually or mechanically. Manual methods involve some labor, and work well for smaller amounts of hashish. Mechanical pressing is very fast, convenient and efficient. However, acquiring the right tool for the job—a good mechanical press—requires an investment of a few hundred dollars. This section describes the best manual methods and then offers some resources for mechanical pressing.

Hot Bottle Pressing

Bubble Man, maker of Bubble Bags®, has surveyed hash-pressing techniques to find the most efficient ones. He prefers a manual technique that he learned from a Moroccan man who had been smoking hash for decades. This method works well for pressing water hash and kief.

EQUIPMENT

- Food-grade cellophane or turkey cooking bags
- Cardboard
- Masking tape
- Newspaper
- Frying pan
- Stove
- Heavy-duty gloves or cooking mitts
- Funnel
- Large empty glass bottle (a wine bottle is perfect, some oil bottles will work)
- Cork or lid for bottle
- Boiling water
- Well-dried kief or water hash
- Small piece of marble slate (cutting board size)

Method

Cut a small piece of cardboard that will serve as backing for the hash block. It should be sized to accommodate the amount of material you have—usually a few inches wide by a few inches long. Make sure to use food-grade cellophane to avoid melting plastics into your smoking material. Wrap the cardboard in cellophane or place it in

DECARBOXYLATION EXPLAINED

Some THC in resin is present in the form THC-A, also called THC acid. This form of THC has a carbonate molecule (COOH) attached to it, which is also called a carboxyl group or acid. THC is only marginally psychoactive when a carboxyl group is attached.

To decarboxylate is to remove the carbonate molecule. This simply means breaking the bond between the COOH molecule and the THC molecule. This is usually accomplished through mild heat.

When the carbonate molecule is removed from THC acid, the COOH evaporates away in the form of water vapor (H_2O) and carbon dioxide (CO_2), and THC is left behind. Converting THC-A through decarboxylation improves the available THC content, sometimes called "potentiating" the THC. The potency is increased because more psychoactive elements are available.

the turkey bag, and cut two sides so the bag is a little bit bigger than the cardboard piece.

Fold over the cut sides of the bag and tape them securely so that it is completely sealed on three sides. Masking tape works best because it won't come loose when the packet is heated or when it comes into contact with steam. Only one side remains open.

Next tap your bone-dry material into the open side of the pack. You can use a rolled-up piece of paper for a funnel. Fill the bag along one side of the cardboard. Once the bag is filled, the top is also sealed with tape. Leave a

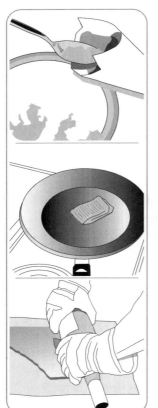

little air in the bag so it doesn't pop under pressure. Some people put a few pinholes in the cellophane to make sure it doesn't burst like a balloon when pressure is placed on it.

Soak a few full sheets of newspaper in water and wrap them around the packet. Put the wrapped packet in a frying pan that is placed on the lowest possible setting on the stove. If the heat is too intense, it can ruin the hash. Keep the newspaper wet. The wet paper combined with the low heat steams the packet and causes the glands to gently melt and stick together.

Turn the packet occasionally so that both sides get equal time. Depending on the size, the packet is heated in this way for a half hour to an hour and a half. Even though it is on a low heat setting, don't forget about it! If you do, the newspaper will dry out and could catch on fire. It will probably have to be rewetted every 15 to 30 minutes. If you are prone to walk off and forget it, set a kitchen timer or alarm clock for every ten minutes while the packet is on the stove, so it will remind you to go back and check.

About 15 minutes before the end of the cooking time, turn the oven on to 350 degrees. Place the piece of marble slab in the oven. Then put a quart of water in a pot on the stovetop to boil.

Take the packet out after it has heated for the proper amount of time and peel back the newspaper to see if it has all melted evenly. Remember, it has been over low heat; it may be a little warm to the touch. Now it's time to press.

Using a funnel, fill the empty wine bottle with the boiling water from the pot on the stovetop. Do this in the sink, bathtub, or outside to avoid spilling boiling water everywhere.

Select a space on a hard floor surface. Concrete floors in a garage or basement are good choices, since it is unlikely that these floors will be damaged by spills, breakage or heat. If working on a linoleum or tile floor, evenly layer dry newspaper or magazines to create a buffer for the hot marble. Take out the heated up marble slab and place on the selected surface.

Place the packet still wrapped in paper on the warm marble working surface. Handle the bottle with gloves because it should be hot to the touch. Press the packet with the water-filled bottle, starting in the middle and working out in all directions. It takes around a half hour, depending on the size of the packet, to press the material.

Once you are done pressing the piece, remove the newspaper wrapping. It is optimal to place the piece in the freezer and allow it to cool and solidify so the cellophane peels off easily. A half-hour to an hour should be long enough. The heat will have darkened the color of the hash.

VARIATIONS ON THE HOT BOTTLE METHOD
After the material is packaged in cellophane and wrapped in wet newspaper, there are a few variations on how it can be heated and pressed to achieve good results:

- Instead of heating the material on the stove, it can be heated using an iron. Set the iron to a warm setting. Irons can get very hot and the wrong setting could ruin the material. Press the material lightly, turning it so that each side is heated equally for 5-15 minutes per side depending on the size of the packet.

- Instead of using a bottle filled with boiling water, a rolling pin can be used to roll out the material. A regular rolling pin works fine, but it will not have the added benefit of heat. Heavy marble rolling pins work best, and so long as there are not combustible or meltable parts (i.e., the handles), a marble rolling pin could be warmed in the oven along with the marble slab to incorporate heat and improve the rolling process.

Shoe Hash

This pressing method lets you multi-task. While you are busy doing other things, the hash is being inconspicuously pressed within your shoe!

Shoe hash is a low-hassle way to press small amounts of kief or water hash. A few grams, usually 5 grams or less, is bagged in a sealed cellophane or plastic bag from which nearly all the air has been squeezed out. The bag seal can be reinforced with tape. Some people like to double bag. Obviously, it is important for scientific as well as psychological reasons to be sure the material is securely sealed since it is going in your shoe.

It is then wrapped in light fabric or a layer of newspaper. This secured package is placed inside a shoe that the hash-maker is planning to wear. Some shoes allow for the kief to be placed between a support insert and the bottom of the shoe. Hard-soled shoes or boots are better for pressing than soft-soled shoes, such as sports shoes.

The rubbing of the heel within the shoe, aided by body heat, presses the hash into a slab. The pressing takes at least an hour of on-foot activity, but it benefits from additional wear.

Some people heat the material as described in the hot-bottle pressing method before shoe pressing.

Pressing by Hand

Pressing by hand is an often-described method to transform kief into hashish a few grams at a time. Fresh hand-rubbed resin is often pressed by hand too, at least initially.

While pressing by hand is convenient since it requires no additional equipment, it does take considerable energy and the results are better with a practiced technique. Those unaccustomed to hand pressing may find it difficult to make the material cohere. The considerable work it takes to get well-pressed hash can easily result in sore hands.

This method works best using medium to high quality material that has been freshly sieved. Kief will be more difficult to mold into hashish and may not stick together properly if a significant amount of vegetative material is present.

To hand press, measure out a small mound of fresh kief. A few grams are usually the most that will fit comfortably in the hand. This material is worked with one hand against the other until it begins to cohere into a solid piece. Then it is rubbed between the palms, or between finger and thumb. The material will begin to change in density. Producing a solid piece of hashish usually requires at least 10 minutes of work when hand pressing. Dry, aged kief will lack some of its original stickiness and may take longer to stick together, but if it was stored properly it should cooperate, even though it may require more kneading. When a piece of hashish has not been pressed properly, it will crumble easily at room temperature.

If the kief is particularly stubborn and won't stick together to form a mass, it can be mildly heated. This can be done in the same way as for other methods: Wrap the material in food-grade cellophane, ensuring that it is completely sealed and all the air is squeezed out. Then wrap this package in several layers of thoroughly wetted newspaper. Warm, turning frequently, in a skillet that is set on lowest heat. It doesn't need to be heated as long as other methods. In hand pressing, the point of heating is to get the material to stick together so it can be kneaded into a solid piece.

Another method is to wrap it in the same manner and press it for a few seconds on each side with an iron that is set on a very low heat setting.

Machine Presses

Making hash is a cinch with a mechanical press. Most presses cost over $100, with high-end models priced at $300 and up. Bookbinding presses, called nipping presses, can be used. Plans are available on the web for building a press using a hydraulic jack.

Hand-pumped hydraulic presses are a less expensive way to get a tight press. Another cost-effective method uses a vice grip, although it will take some adaptation. For small amounts, Space Case® just released a new Pollen Press, which may be used in conjunction with their handheld kief-collecting grinder. Kief or thoroughly dried water hash is added to this small metal tube. The tension pin is placed in, and the pollen press is screwed shut. The next day, the kief has been pressed into a neat hash block. This tool is a very affordable option at $35. See the resource section for information on purchasing this and other mechanical presses.

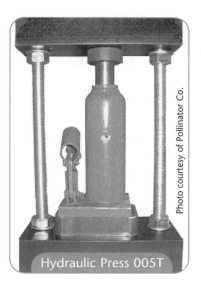

Hydraulic Press 005T

Photo courtesy of Pollinator Co.

STORAGE

The beginning of the chapter pointed out that loose material—kief or unpressed water hash—tolerates storage better than hash. Pressing exposes THC to air and also potentiates THC through decarboxylation—changing THC-A to THC using mild heat. The hashmaking process is thought to improve the quality and complexity of the high, but it also makes the material more vulnerable to deterioration.

Once the hashish is pressed, it can still be kept for months or possibly years, with little deterioration to its potency and flavor if storage is handled properly. A frost-free freezer is the best place for storing hash.

Glass containers are preferable for storage. Plastics and rubber are not recommended because the terpenes—responsible for the flavor and aroma of the hash—are somewhat volatile compounds that interact chemically with plastic or rubber, degrading both the hash and the container.

Over time, the outer layer of hashish has lower potency than the inside, since it is exposed to higher levels of light and oxygen. Studies suggest that dark-colored hash degrades more rapidly than hash that is lighter in color. Remember that mild heat darkens the hash? Part of the reason the color changes is that more glands have been broken in forming the hash, leaving them less protected from light, heat, moisture and oxygen—the main contributors to deterioration.

RESOURCES

Mechanical Presses:

Longevity Herb Company
Several models are available.
1549 West Jewett Boulevard
White Salmon, WA 98672
509-493-2626
avery@gorge.net

Pollinator Company
The Pollinator Company
carries the Hydraulic Press
005T (pictured, page 89).
Cornelis Trooststraat 37
Postbus 76175
1070 ED, Amsterdam
The Netherlands
+31 20 470-8889
+31 20 471-5242 fax
info@pollinator.nl
www.pollinator.nl

Space Case® Pollen Press
Full Circle Distribution, Inc.
P.O. Box 2486
Capistrano Beach, CA 92624
949-369-8388
949-369-8384 fax
info@orangechronic.com
www.orangechronic.com

Make-Your-Own Hash Press
See Ot1's Homebuilt
Hash Press article in the
magazine archives at
www.overgrow.com
(http://www.overgrow.com/
articles/3). This method has
not been tested and is provided only as a resource.
Those interested in building
their own press will have to
make an assessment as to
the accuracy of these
instructions and assume their
own risk in following them.

Cannabis produces THC glands on the leaves and bracts as well as the buds.

A close-up inspection with a magnifying glass or photographer's loupe reveals droplet-shaped trichomes that rest on the ends of small, hair-like stems. Material with visible glands is worth keeping.

Photos: C.P.O.

Photo: Ed Rosenthal

Photo: Ed Rosenthal

When saving leaf and trim, the stems are removed and the material is thoroughly dried. Some methods call for further processing. Before making tinctures, capsules, water hash or food dishes, the material may be snipped or ground to a more manageable consistency.

Right: After the valuable glands have been removed, the leaf is tossed out.

Photo: Ed Rosenthal

92

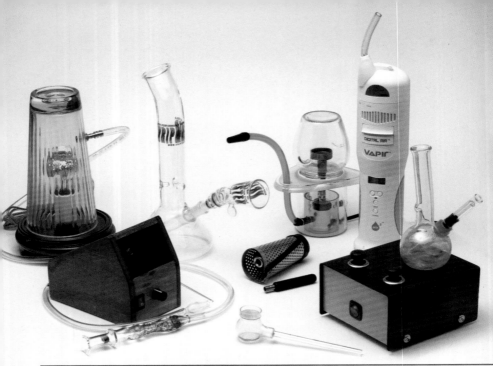

Vaporizers come in many shapes and sizes, but they all operate by heating the bud or kief to a temperature which releases THC vapors without burning the plant material. All vaporizers pictured here are discussed in chapter 2.

Below: The Tulip™ vaporizer acquires a red glow when in use.

Above: Grinders like the ones pictured here from Sweetleaf™ make it easy to prepare the material for vaporizing. Grinding is an important step because it improves the exposed surface of the bud and optimizes air flow for a smooth running machine.

Courtesy of Quick Trading

Kief is a snap
to make with the right
tools. Pictured here: Wire mesh
framed in wood makes a great home-
made sifter; Pocket-sized grinder/pollen catcher
from Space Case® salvages glands that escape during grinding; Whiskey Falls Crystal Catcher® sorts and stores material.

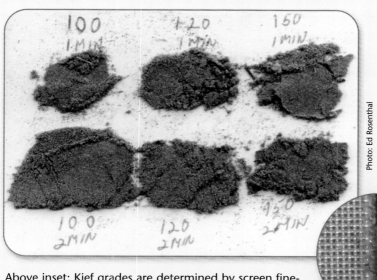

Photo: Ed Rosenthal

Courtesy of Bubble Man

Above inset: Kief grades are determined by screen fine-
ness and sifting time. The pictured material was sifted on
3 screen sizes for either one or two minutes. The top right
sample (150 for 1 minute) is the lightest and purest.

60x magnification

Right inset: Sometimes, size does matter: 77-micron wire mesh (left) is compared here with mesh that measures 212 microns between wires (right).

The Tumble Now® machine makes dry sift hash or kief using a rotating 125 micron stainless steel cylinder. The dry sift can then be separated into 2 grades using the included 70 micron screen.

Bubble Bags® at work:
1. First, plant trimmings, ice and water are added to a bucket lined with Bubble Bags.
2. The mixture is stirred for 15 to 20 minutes.
3. The bags are pulled out one by one, collecting each grade of hash separately. The 73 and 90 micron bags usually make the best hash.

Bubble Now® machines perform the mixing part of the water extraction process. Its gentle agitation produces top quality Bubble Hash every time.

The Bubble Bags® system is available in three sizes to suit individual processing needs and preferences. The manageable one-gallon bags are pictured in action here (left top and center). Above: Twenty-gallon systems allow a bulk of material to be processed at one time. The standard, five-gallon system is shown in chapter 4.

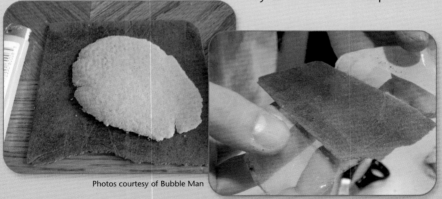

Above left: The fruits of the labor: water hash produced using the Bubble Bags® system. This photo shows the dramatic effect pressing method can have on hash color. The top piece was hand-pressed, while the piece on which it rests was pressed using heat.

Above right: This fine specimen is unwrapped from its cellophane after being pressed using the hot bottle method explained in chapter 5.

Top right and left: Material before and after pressing.

Below: When hash is good quality, it should soften from the warmth of your hands.

Left: An impressive selection of hash from Amsterdam's Bluebird coffeeshop shows the many colors and shapes hash can take depending on the material and pressing method used.

Photo: Ed Rosenthal

Making butter in a double boiler keeps the material from burning without adding water to the mix. This potent mixture is almost ready for straining.

Mouthwatering edibles with a kick from some of California's talented medical marijuana bakers. Cookies and other snack-sized foods are perfect candidates for cannabization.

Courtesy of Quick Trading

CHAPTER

6

TINCTURES

WHAT exactly is a tincture? While the word sounds obscure and complicated, the method of preparation is anything but. Actually, the word *tincture* derives from the Latin and simply means a colored herbal extract. A tincture is a concentrated solution of an herb in liquid, usually a mix of alcohol and water. It is often packaged in a dropper bottle and is taken by squeezing out droplets on or under the tongue.

Tinctures are potent and safe herbal medicines. Echinacea and St. John's Wort are two of the most popular extracts available on health-care shelves. When cannabis was still a part of Western medical practice in the early 20th century, tinctures were the most common medicinal preparation.

Making tinctures is low-tech and requires more patience than effort. A speedy method that can be completed in a day is offered, but it may not be as pleasing to the connoisseur as the slower, traditional method. The traditional method takes one to two months to finish.

Other methods of marijuana processing, such as cooking, offer more immediately gratifying results. However, tincture making is fairly low maintenance compared to these methods. It also has the advantage of a long shelf life. It is relatively easy to start and not very cumbersome to store. So long as the instructions for keeping and maintaining it are followed, tinctures can be left for months after the process is started, and then completed when it is convenient or when the stash is running low.

TINCTURE CHEMISTRY

Making a tincture is not so different than making a cup of tea. Think of tea. Boiling water is added to a mixture of leaves, flowers or roots. These plant parts have substances that are soluble in water. The water-soluble pigments and other plant qualities create the flavor and color of the tea, as well as its phyto-active or health-enhancing chemicals, such as the active protectants in Echinacea. The tea leaves are removed, and the result is a beverage with the flavor and qualities of the plants used to make it.

Cannabis tinctures are very similar. The big difference is that they are not infused in water. This is because THC and other cannabinoids contained in marijuana are not water soluble—that is, they do not dissolve in water. They can be released using other compounds, such as alcohol or glycerin when making tinctures, or oil when used for cooking.

Put simply, a tincture is made by soaking parts of the marijuana plant in a base that *extracts* the THC and other cannabinoids, separating them from the plant material and dissolving them into the alcohol or glycerin base. Heat is kept low if it is used at all. The plant material is removed after it has been given a chance to infuse. The active ingredients of the plant have dissolved into the base. The result is then bottled, and voila: tincture.

The Effects and Effectiveness of Tinctures

Tinctures are administered by dropper under the tongue, or "sublingually." The cannabinoids are absorbed by the mucous membranes under the tongue and elsewhere in the mouth and upper throat. They are released into the bloodstream and do not pass through the digestive system. This is an advantage for two reasons. When substances pass through the digestive system, both in food and to a lesser extent in alcohol, it takes a minimum of 25 minutes to start feeling their effects.

The digestive system is not as efficient as sublingual transmission into the bloodstream. Food must pass through the liver in the last stage of digestion. This organ filters out poisons and other unusual substances that have passed through the intestines and stomach on the way to the bloodstream. It also filters out a portion of the cannabinoids, so they never reach your bloodstream or your brain.

It is easy to figure out titration, the scientific term for dosage, using tinctures sublingually. The high begins about five minutes after taking the tincture. Full effects are felt about 20 minutes after dosage. Tinctures vary in potency and effect from batch to batch. This is partly the result of different makers' recipes for the process. Using bud, trim and leaf in different ratios produces tinctures of varying

strengths. Marijuana varieties differ in effect, and the quality and amount used determine the potency of the tincture.

Historically, the variability of potency hindered the use of cannabis extracts as a modern medicine because it made tinctures impossible to standardize. This was one of the main reasons given for the removal of cannabis from the pharmacoepia in the early 20th century. For the home tincture-maker, consistency is less of an issue. When prepared at home in one batch or in many small batches from the same plant material, the tincture maker has an easier time finding a consistently good titration.

Some people say that tinctures don't affect them much or don't produce the full spectrum of desired effects for medicinal or recreational purposes. Sad to say, but these people just haven't run across a well-made tincture from grass worth extracting. A well-made extract is both a very pleasant and effective way to administer cannabinoids without smoking.

Advantages

Cannabis tinctures deliver the effects of smoking with just a short delay. Since they are not burned, no tars or other pyrolytic compounds are inhaled.

With no smoke, the use of the herb is unobtrusive. The bottle looks like a regular over-the-counter medicine. There is no tell-tale smoke produced, and nobody smells or notices as you self-titrate. The "no smoking" sign is of little consequence to your plans. There is no bulky equipment, and no fire is required.

The Proper Dose

Once you have experienced a particular batch a few times, you will find it easy to figure out the right dose.

Each person's tolerance to tincture is different, just as people's tolerance to the smoked product differs. To be on the safe side, start with small doses, adjusting upward as necessary. A good starter dosage for the recipes provided here is about $1/2$ of a dropper of tincture. Tincture doses typically range between the contents of one dropper (approximately 30-40 drops) and six droppers. Since both the potency of tinctures and people's tolerances differ, there is no way to prescribe a definite dose, only a range to suggest.

MAKING TINCTURES

The Three Phases of Tincture Making

In the first phase of tincture making, the ingredients are combined. In the middle phase, the mixture is occasionally agitated, and then allowed to sit until the THC has been absorbed into the base. In the last phase, the plant material is strained out, and the tincture is bottled. One person can easily accomplish the first two phases, but a second set of hands makes the last phase easier. Following traditional methods, the entire process takes at least a month for alcohol tinctures and two months for glycerin tinctures. For convenience, the tincture can be left in phase two indefinitely, as long as it is maintained. Some connoisseurs prefer the mellower flavor that results from aging. A speedier tincture recipe is offered as well, for those who can't wait out the traditional methods.

BUZZ BEE'S ALCOHOL TINCTURE

Buzz Bee, who provides tinctures to medical dispensaries in California, has shared her methods and tips.

EQUIPMENT

- 3% hydrogen peroxide rinse (see box, p.105) brewer's non-sudsing detergent or antibacterial dishsoap
- One 1-gallon, large-mouth amber glass jar with lid
- One 1-gallon, small-mouth amber glass jar with lid
- Several dropper bottles
- Large bowl
- Funnel
- 2-4 pastry cloths big enough to line above bowl
- A clean, wet dish towel and a few clean dry towels or paper towels dedicated to clean-up (they will likely be stained after use)
- Pump with tubing for small-mouth jar
- Disposable latex or neoprene gloves

INGREDIENTS

- Alcohol: Korbel Brandy (approximately three 750-ml bottles)
- 8 cups prepared trim mixture

NOTES ON INGREDIENTS

- Buzz Bee uses these proportions as her recipe:
    4 cups (1 quart) shake
    2 cups A+ trim
    1-2 oz. indica or sativa bud
- These amounts fill a gallon jar. The completed amount will be approximately 1/2 of a gallon jar.
- The amount of brandy may vary, depending on the plant material used. The best tinctures are made from the highest quality material.
- Kief can also be used, but is better used separately rather than as part of the trim mixture. See kief tincture, p. 116.

BUZZ BEE'S TIPS:

- **Amber-colored jars** are best because they block light, which degrades THC. If amber jars cannot be obtained, then clear glass jars can be used, but they should be kept in the dark. It is best to have at least two jars for each recipe being made. Buzz Bee recommends one wide-mouth jar and one small-mouth jar per batch. The lids must create a complete seal.

- **Dropper bottles** should be amber or blue glass. They can be found at health food, herbal, or science supply stores. They are also easily found on the web. They come in a number of sizes, commonly ranging from $1/2$ oz. to 4 oz. bottles.

- **Hydrogen peroxide** is a great sterilizer. To make a rinse from 3% hydrogen peroxide, combine ten ounces per quart of water.

- **Please Note!** Pastry cloth and cheesecloth are two different things altogether. If you try to use cheese cloth, you are signing up for a frustrating experience. Cheesecloth will allow plant parts through and there will be plant material in the tincture after the straining process.

Phase One: Starting the Process

First don the gloves so that you don't irritate your hands with the harsh cleanser. Using lab detergent cleanser, available at brewing shops, wash all the jars and the rest of the equipment. Make sure to rinse the equipment thoroughly.

After everything is washed, fill the gallon jar with prepared trash. When all the trash is in the jar, it should be $3/4$ full. If the trash being processed is particularly potent, less can be used. The converse is true with weaker cannabis.

Phase Two: Agitate and Wait

During the two-month waiting period, shake the jar once a day for five minutes. If the liquid level drops, add more brandy to keep the liquid at two inches below the top.

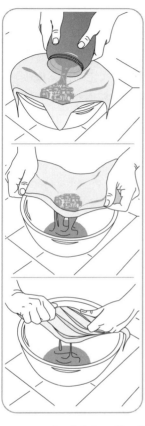

Phase Three: Straining and Bottling

The final steps consist of straining the plant material out and bottling the extract for use.

It is now time to get out the rest of the equipment. The cleanser, the jar of mixture, the small-mouth gallon jar, large mixing bowl, funnel, and pastry cloth are gathered on a clean and clear working surface.

Again, all materials need to be cleaned. Hands should be gloved using disposable latex or neoprene gloves.

Line the bowl with a pastry cloth so that the edges hang over the sides of the bowl. The cloth must be big enough so that the edges will not submerge once the mixture is poured into the bowl. Pour the mixture into the bowl on top of the cloth. The pastry cloth is the strainer; make sure it does not dip into the bowl, which will allow plant material to slip through. This step can be done in batches to avoid spillover. The bowl should only be filled about 2/3 of the way full. The tincture mixture is very green from concentrated chlorophyll and stains anything that it touches. Keep clean towels on hand for quick clean-up of any spills.

The ends of the pastry cloth are carefully brought together so that no plant material can escape. The cloth is lifted above the bowl and allowed to drip into it. The plant material should all be inside the cloth. Taking care to bunch the cloth so that all trash is trapped inside, the pastry cloth

TINCTURE LIFE SPAN   ASK ED

Ed:

A friend of mine has tincture that is three years old. She insists that since the tincture is made with alcohol, it is still good. Can tinctures stay good that long? Will they go bad or become weaker over time?

How much tincture should a normal dose be?

Thanks, Tincture Curious

Ann Arbor, Michigan

Curious:

Tinctures are usually made with alcohol, and so long as they are stored properly, they can keep indefinitely. The main dangers to tincture are light and oxygen, which both degrade THC content. For this reason, the best way to store a tincture is in an opaque container in the freezer. Dark glass is best.

Oxygen breaks THC down into non-psychoactive components, so long exposure to the air will reduce the potency of a tincture. It is necessary to keep tincture in a sealed container. This also prevents contamination of the material.

If the tincture was diluted with water, and the water was not distilled, the tincture can turn sour. This should be apparent. You won't enjoy the smell or taste because it will be obviously sour, like vinegar.

Tinctures that have been properly stored and aged often take on a mellower flavor that many connoisseurs enjoy.

is wrung out over the bowl, and then placed aside.* What remains in the bowl should be a slightly tinted liquid clear of plant debris. This is the tincture.

You might find it easier to separate the tincture from the residue using a large metal strainer. It doesn't require quite the finesse that using the cloth does. Make sure to press or squeeze as much liquid as you can from the leaves.

---

*Note: You can discard the plant material or keep it and use it as a poultice for external injuries.

Buzz Bee pours her material from the bowl into a small-mouth, one-gallon amber glass jug. This is where a funnel comes in handy. Pour the tincture from the bowl into the jar.

The new jar won't be full because the plant material has been removed. Buzz Bee uses a small-mouth jug because she can then insert a pump like those found on ketchup cans to easily fill dropper bottles. After filling the desired number of dropper bottles, any remaining tincture can be stored in this jug. The pump is removed, and the jar is sealed and stored in a dark, cool place. Every time droppers are filled, the pump and jars should be clean.

BUZZ BEE'S NON-ALCOHOL TINCTURE
Why Glycerin?

If the idea of tinctures is appealing, but the alcohol is not, food-grade glycerin can replace alcohol as the base. Nutritionally, glycerin is a sugar, but its chemical structure looks like a sugar base with an alcohol molecule attached. Glycerin has extracting/emulsifying properties, but is a weaker extractor than alcohol. This means that material must be left longer in a glycerin base to make an equally potent product. Food-grade glycerin is available at many natural food stores, home-brewing supply stores or on the web.

EQUIPMENT

- Brewing equipment sanitizer, 3% hydrogen peroxide rinse (see box, p. 105) or antibacterial dish soap
- One 1-gallon, large-mouth amber glass jar with lid
- One 1-gallon, small-mouth amber glass jar with lid
- Several dropper bottles
- A clean, wet dish towel and a few clean dry towels or

paper towels that can be sacrificed to clean-up (they
will likely be stained after use)
- Pump with tubing for small-mouth jar
- Disposable latex or neoprene gloves

FOR MANUAL SIEVING
- Large bowl
- Funnel
- Pastry cloth big enough to line above bowl

FOR PRESS SIEVING
- Wine or fruit press
- Mesh bag (may come with press)

INGREDIENTS
- Approximately $1/2$ to 1 gal. food-grade glycerin
- 8 cups prepared trim mixture

NOTES ON INGREDIENTS
- Buzz Bee uses material in these proportions:
  4 cups (1 quart) shake
  2 cups A+ trim
  1-2 oz. indica or sativa bud
- These amounts fill a gallon jar.
- The amount of glycerin may vary, depending on the
  type of trash used.
- Kief can also be used, but is better used separately rather
  than as part of the trim mixture. See kief tincture, p. 116.

Phase One: Getting Started

To start, you only need the large-mouth amber jar, the
cleanser and the ingredients. Cleanliness is the majority of

the work and the key ingredient to success in the first part of the process. Brewing equipment sanitizer or hydrogen peroxide rinse is used to clean all utensils and jars that are being used. Hands must also be clean. Disposable neoprene or latex gloves are recommended.

Add a little glycerin to the jar first, then add the plant material. Because glycerin is thicker than alcohol, this will make mixing easier. Once all the trash is in the jar, glycerin is added until the jar is nearly full. Leave about an inch at the top for agitation. Label the jar with the date and any other pertinent information, such as the variety of marijuana or the trash recipe used.

Phase Two: Agitate and Wait

Store the jar in a warm, dark place where you won't entirely forget about it. You need to remember it often enough to shake the jar daily for five minutes. This phase takes a minimum of two months, but it can be longer. The glycerin method takes twice as long as alcohol because the chemical process is weaker.

Phase Three: Ready for Bottling

When two months have elapsed, the plant material can be strained out. The strained tincture is then bottled for use.

Sieving Manually

For first-time or one-time tincture makers, the traditional method of using a large mixing bowl, funnel, and pastry cloth is the most cost-effective route. Glycerin is thicker and is more difficult than alcohol to sieve by hand.

Gather the remaining equipment. This includes cleanser, the tincture mixture, the small-mouth gallon jar, towels,

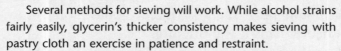

IDEAS FOR SIEVING

Several methods for sieving will work. While alcohol strains fairly easily, glycerin's thicker consistency makes sieving with pastry cloth an exercise in patience and restraint.

Other materials that could be used for straining or in the construction of a special tincture sieve include:

- fruit/wine press mesh bags
- a new clean set of nylon panty hose
- silk-screening material
- fine wire mesh
- a potato ricer
- hops bags used in beer brewing

a large mixing bowl, funnel, pump and dropper bottles. Pastry cloth or clean panty hose can be used as the sieve.

Create a sanitary working surface and clean all equipment to be used. Line the bowl with the pastry cloth so that the edges hang over the sides of the bowl (see illustration, p. 106). The cloth should cover the entire bowl. If the edges submerge in the mixture and let plant material through, the tincture will have to be re-sieved.

Pour some of the tincture mixture into the bowl on top of the cloth. The bowl should only be filled about 1/2 to 2/3 of the way full. The glycerin is slightly gooey and will strain more slowly through the pastry cloth than the alcohol does. It will also absorb readily into the cloth. The cloth must be handled carefully when wrung out to avoid ripping. The tincture mixture is very green and stains anything that it touches.

Bring the ends of the pastry cloth together so that no plant material can escape. The plant material should all be inside the cloth. Taking care to bunch the cloth so that all

trash is trapped inside, the pastry cloth is wrung out over the bowl, and then placed aside.* What remains in the bowl should be a slightly tinted, gooey liquid clear of plant debris. This is the tincture.

Pour the tincture from the bowl into the small-mouth, one-gallon amber glass jug using a funnel. Repeat this process until all of the tincture has been sieved, using a clean, dry pastry cloth each time. Re-using the same cloth may cause it to rip and the entire tincture will have to be filtered again.

The new jar will not be full because the plant material has been removed. Buzz Bee dilutes the glycerin tincture with water because it is otherwise too thick to pass through the dropper. She recommends a ratio of one part water to two parts tincture. Once the tincture is diluted, Buzz Bee uses the pump to fill the dropper bottles. She labels and dates the bottles so as not to confuse them. This also helps identify proper dosages for different batches.

Sieving with a Press

Buzz Bee has had plenty of experience making batches of non-alcohol tincture, and she sang high praises for using a fruit or wine press when making this tincture at regular intervals or in large quantities. Fruit or wine presses can be found at brewery or winemaking supply stores, at stores that offer canning or fruit processing supplies, or on the web.

There are a lot of fancy presses out there designed for the wine snob, but they are expensive and unnecessary for the purposes of tincture making, and may even be unsuitable for this use. The best tincture press is basic. A system

---

Note: You can discard the plant material or keep it and use it as a poultice for external injuries.

that works out of a plastic bucket (illustrated here), like Buzz Bee's does, is ideal. Presses of this type cost around $100. A few retailers who offer simple presses are listed at the end of the chapter.

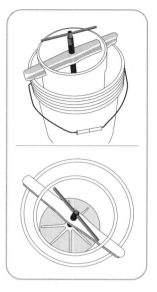

Often, fruit or wine presses will come with a special mesh bag that is very useful. It is also reusable. If the press does not include a mesh bag, one can probably be acquired from the same place where the press was purchased. It's not a bad idea to purchase an extra one for backup.

A press is a precision instrument. It works from the basic principle of applying even pressure. It is not advisable to make a homemade press unless you possess the tools and the ability to figure out and deliver precise measurements.

Follow the instructions that come with the press you purchase. With Buzz Bee's press, the material is poured out of the amber gallon jar into the mesh bag, which is held over the press reservoir. The bag is then squeezed in a vice-like fashion by the press mechanism. The mesh bag is specially designed to allow a thick liquid like glycerin through without risk of tearing. It also squeezes the material with much more strength and less mess than a person can do by hand.

The plant material is easily removed from the press, leaving only the tincture behind. With a funnel, the tincture is poured from the reservoir into a clean, small-mouth gallon jug. It is diluted to a strength of one part water to two parts tincture. Dilution produces a consistency that can be dispensed with a dropper.

The trash in the mesh bag can be thrown out or saved and used as a poultice for external injuries. The bag is washed and sanitized according to the directions supplied with the press.

ASK ED'S SUPER SPEEDY TINCTURE

Traditional recipes for tincture talk about an aging process: "Let the mixture sit for . . . ." The reason that the drink gets stronger as it ages is that more of the THC dissolves in the alcohol as time passes. This method speeds up the process by dissolving the THC from the plant material quickly.

EQUIPMENT

- Laboratory non-sudsing detergent cleanser or 3% hydrogen peroxide rinse (see box, p. 105)
- Disposable neoprene or latex gloves
- Blender
- Metal, serrated serving spoon
- Colander
- Bowl to hold colander
- Fine mesh strainer
- Bowl to go beneath fine mesh strainer
- Metal spoon
- Cloth kitchen towel
- Amber or dark glass jar with lid

INGREDIENTS

- Bud, trim or leaf material
- Grain neutral spirits such as Everclear or overproof alcohol such as 151 rum or vodka.

Method

Clean all the equipment. Weigh the marijuana. Then place it in a colander up to one-third full. Place the colander in a mixing bowl. Do not break up the leaves or buds, so the glands remain on the leaf surfaces. Add enough room-temperature water so that the leaf can spread out in the water. Let it sit in the warm water for an hour or so. This bath will dissolve the non-active, water-soluble pigments and carbohydrates from the plant material.

Strain the plant material. Wearing gloves, roll the material into a ball. Wrap it in a clean towel and press on it to squeeze out as much water as possible.

Place the strained plant material in a blender. Add alcohol at the rate of ten ounces of alcohol per ounce of marijuana. Place the cover on the blender. Turn on the blender at the lowest setting and let it run for five minutes. Let it sit for an hour, then turn the blender on low again for five minutes. Let the mixture sit for a couple of hours so that the leaf floats to the top of the alcohol.

Using a serving spoon, remove the floating debris and put it in the strainer with a bowl underneath to catch the drainage. Then, pressing the grass against the strainer with your gloved hands, squeeze out as much alcohol as you can. Discard the plant material.

Take all the liquid and run it through a fine mesh strainer. The tincture is ready to use, but a little raw. It can now be moved to an amber or dark-colored glass jar that is sealed. Eventually the minute insoluble particles will float on the tincture or sink to the bottom of the jar. They can be removed.

Test the tincture. If it is too strong, add alcohol or water. If it is not strong enough, the tincture can be concentrated a bit by allowing some of the alcohol to

evaporate. This is accomplished by allowing the tincture to sit open in a warm room for a few hours. Better to let it sit in a bowl so that there is greater surface area to speed evaporation. The rate at which the alcohol evaporates varies according to a number of conditions, but a visible difference should occur within a few hours. Longer exposure to warmth and oxygen degrades the THC content and may possibly introduce contaminants. Return the tincture to a clean glass container and seal.

KIEF TINCTURE

Kief, the sifted glands of marijuana (see chapter 3), can easily be used to make a tincture. Because it is free of most of the vegetative material and is quite concentrated, kief makes a very fine extract.

There are several grades of kief. The first sifting is the purest. Each subsequent sift yields a product with more vegetative debris. The first grades are usually used for vaporizing or smoking. The lower grades are best used for cooking and tinctures.

To make a kief tincture, use two grams of kief per ounce of vodka, rum, Everclear or other alcohol. Place the kief in a jar that can be sealed, or in a blender, and then add the alcohol. Cover tightly and shake the jar or let the blender rip. Let stand at least overnight in a warm, dark place. The mixture can be left longer if desired.

Strain the mixture through a paper coffee filter. Transfer the mixture to a clean dropper bottle. It is a good idea to label the bottle as kief tincture and include the date.

STORAGE

Tincture can be stored in the sealed gallon jug or pumped into the desired number of dropper bottles. Thoroughly sanitize empty bottles before refilling them.

Label bottles with the date and tincture information to differentiate batches. Tinctures stay potent indefinitely. The main dangers to a tincture's integrity are heat, light and oxygen. The best storage for a tincture is in a dark-colored glass container that is sealed and kept in a cool, dark place. The freezer is optimal.

GETTING CREATIVE: VARIATIONS
Alcohol

While Buzz Bee recommends brandy, and Ask Ed's speedy tincture requires overproof alcohol, it is possible to use other alcohols instead.

Other suggested alcohols for Buzz Bee's method include high-proof varieties, such as rum, vodka or grain alcohol. Using an alcohol with a higher proof increases the extracting capability. If the results are too harsh or sting the mouth and tongue, dilute the tincture with water.

Buzz Bee prefers brandy for its mellow quality. It doesn't burn and has a taste she finds pleasing. However, it is not as effective a solvent because of its lower alcohol content. In addition, the high percentage of water in the brandy dissolves non-cannabinoid, non-active water solubles such as chlorophyll and other pigments.

Alcohol can be selected for its flavor. Fruit schnapps or flavored brandies have a high enough proof to be effective, giving the tincture a fruity or minty flavor. Using flavored liquors partially masks the cannabis flavor. These beverages are also often colored, so they might hide the

green tint and cannabis smell a bit, producing a more stealth product.

Essences are also available in many flavors and can be added to glycerin tinctures, or to tinctures using unflavored alcohol. These are available through specialty cooking shops or at specialty food sites on the web.

Honey Elixir

Another treat that Buzz Bee makes with her alcohol-based tincture is a honey elixir. Tincture can be transformed into honey elixir right after the straining process is complete, or at a later time. Mix the tincture with honey at a ratio of two parts honey to three parts tincture. The proportions may differ based on how thin or thick the honey is, and should be determined by consistency.

Mildly heat the honey to get a thinner consistency, which makes it easier to work with. The honey and tincture are gently mixed together using a metal spoon or an electric mixer on low speed. Keep the mix free-flowing so the pump can be used to fill the bottles and a dropper still works for administration. Elixir should be stored in the same way as regular tincture.

HONEY ELIXIR TIPS
- When warming the honey don't let it get too hot or the color and chemical properties will change, and it will not mix properly with the tincture.
- When the honey cools, it thickens again. If too high a proportion of honey is mixed with the tincture, the mix will be too thick to use with a dropper once it cools.

Multi-Herbal Tinctures

If medicinal applications are your interest, then combining a cannabis tincture with other herbs or herbal extracts may be worth experimentation.

Many other herbs can be used with marijuana to create a synergistic effect. Valerian root, passion flower, lemon balm, and marjoram are calming, reduce anxiety and aid in sleep. Clove extract can be combined with marijuana tincture for an herbal toothache remedy that is rubbed on the gums.

Additional research into herbal combinations is recommended. Consulting an herbalist may yield a multitude of interesting, personalized extracts.

Cooking with Tincture

Tinctures are also an easy way to cannabinate food. A dropperful in drinks, soups, sauces or mashed potatoes may be just what the doctor ordered. Tinctures mix well with milk drinks such as shakes, Indian lassis or hot chocolate, as well as milk-based sauces.

See chapter 8 for more ideas about how to use tinctures in cooking, or invent recipes of your own. Remember that eating tincture is a different process of assimilation, and dosage will have to be reconsidered.

A LAST NOTE ABOUT DOSAGE

Tinctures are a great option for both medicinal and recreational use. They eliminate all of the negatives regarding smoking and the inconvenience of using a vaporizer.

Dosage varies by the individual. It will be necessary to experiment, and it is advisable to err on the side of caution until the tincture's effect on your head and body is known.

The recommended initial dosage is half a dropperful. Dosages typically range between one full dropper (30-40) drops and six droppers, depending on individual tolerance and the potency of the tincture.

RESOURCES

Tincture Bottles: _____

Specialty Bottle
206-340-0459
service@specialtybottle.com
www.specialtybottle.com

Garden Medicinals
434-964-9113
www.gardenmedicinals.com

Botanical.com
This web site also sells some useful accessorites, such as funnels and large muslin filtering bags for tea.
www.botanical.com

Presses: _____

Herbal Tincture Press
Dept. MR 486
Rich Gulch Rd.
Mokelumne Hill, CA 95245
209-286-1232
209-286-1386 fax

Longevity Herb Company
1549 West Jewett Blvd.
White Salmon, WA 98672
509-493-2626
avery@gorge.net

Midwest Supplies
888-449-2739
www.midwestsupplies.com

Karp's Homebrew Shop
631-261-1235
www.homebrewshop.com

Flavor Extracts: _____

Herb Cupboard
herb@herbcupboard.com
www.herbcupboard.com

7

CAPSULES

MAYBE you've wondered if it were possible to make a marijuana pill. Just pop it in your mouth with a gulp of water and enjoy the therapeutic and mind-enhancing effects of cannabis. Marijuana capsules, or "maripills" are very effective and quite easy to make.

Some people really enjoy the high that results from eating marijuana, but cannabinated foods are not always predictable. Maripills can be a convenient alternative. Medical marijuana patients may find capsules more effective than smoking for pain management. Recent studies suggest that cannabis has stronger analgesic and anti-inflammatory qualities when eaten.

Marijuana capsules begin to take effect 30-90 minutes after being eaten. It is easier to monitor the exact amount of cannabis that is being ingested. Psychoactive effects

typically last 5 to 8 hours, but the herb's medicinal effects may continue for as long as 12 hours.

Because maripills allow cannabis to be eaten without food, these capsules give the individual more choices. When taken on an empty stomach, the high is likely to come on more quickly, and may be more potent. When eaten following a meal, assimilation is slower and the effect is mellower but lasts longer. Medical users may find this increased control over effects reassuring.

The first step in making marijuana capsules is grinding plant material to a powder. This is mixed with cooking oil and heated mildly to potentiate the THC. Once the material has been processed, it is packed into gelatin capsules using a small, inexpensive capsule-filling device.

Gelatin capsules and capsule-filling machines are available at many health food stores. A few resources for these items are offered at the end of the chapter. Capsule-filling machines are small (about the size of a brick) and inexpensive (under $40). They simply hold the gelatin capsule in place, allowing many pills to be made at one time.

It should be noted that gelatin capsules are not vegetarian—they are made from cows. Vegetarian capsules are available, but some types are inadvisable for this process, because they dissolve when exposed to oil. Ask a salesperson if the vegetarian capsules they offer can tolerate an oil-based filling before purchasing them for maripill use.

Size 0 capsules are recommended. This size is not too cumbersome to swallow, and can hold 325 milligrams of marijuana. Dosage may vary between 1 and 5 capsules, depending on the potency of the material used. For people who can tolerate larger capsules, the 00 size is also an option. This size has a capacity of 650 milligrams. Usually 1-2 pills at this size comprise a sufficient dose.

MARIPILLS AND MARINOL®

Marinol® is the brand name given to dronabinol, which consists of synthetic delta-9 THC in a sesame oil base. This is the only cannabis-based medicine currently legal and available by prescription.

Some patients experience good results when using Marinol® but others find that it produces anxiety, or overwhelms them with its strong psychoactivity. Marinol® isolates marijuana's strongest psychoactive component, THC, from other cannabinoids.

Current research confirms what many anecdotes have already suggested: marijuana's other cannabinoids, including cannabidiol (CBD), cannabinol (CBN) and possibly cannabichromine (CBC), work synergistically with THC to produce medically beneficial effects. CBD, for example, has sedative or relaxing properties that counterbalance the stimulating or anxiety-producing qualities of THC.

Since dronabinol does not contain these additional cannabinoids, it not only lacks the analgesic or anti-inflammatory effects that other cannabinoids may offer, but it also loses the complexity that natural marijuana possesses.

Marinol® does of course, have one irrefutable upside—it has passed muster with the Food and Drug Administration and can be prescribed and possessed legally. As a patented medicine, dosage is standardized to a degree that homemade preparations are incapable of matching. Uneven absorption can still be a problem with Marinol®.

It is presently approved, in a limited way, for use in AIDS, cancer and some eating disorders. Marinol® is effective for appetite stimulation, the use for which it was approved. Broader therapeutic applications might be possible when cannabis-derived drugs include multiple cannabinoids. Additional cannabis-derived medicines are currently being researched and developed.

In the meantime, one option for getting full-spectrum cannabinoids is to make products from the source: plant material. The homemade maripills discussed in this chapter are made from leaf, trim or bud, and offer the complete range of cannabinoids. Unlike patented pills, homemade marijuana capsules will vary in potency from batch to batch, and the dosage should be tested and adjusted each time new capsules are made.

HOW TO MAKE MARIPILLS

Maripills can be made from leaf and trim only, bud only or a leaf/bud combination. No matter what is used, it is necessary to process the material before the capsules are filled. Marijuana is soluble in fats, oils and alcohol. It is not soluble in water. In this process, oil is used to prepare the cannabinoids for absorption. Alcohol cannot be used because it will dissolve the gelatin.

Mild heat and oil potentiate the THC, making it easier for the body to utilize it. This processing also makes the material easier to digest. When whole plant material is used, it contains not only the bulbous THC-containing glands, but also the microscopic—and sharp—hairs on which they rest. Oil and heat soften these hairs, making them less irritable to the stomach.

Some people find that even after processing, they have trouble digesting pills that use leaf material exclusively. If this is the case, try using bud or kief. Both kief and bud contain much less vegetative matter than does leaf material. The tiny hairs from the vegetative matter are most likely the culprits in digestive complaints.

EQUIPMENT AND INGREDIENTS

- Cooking oil (olive or canola)
- Plant material (bud, leaf, trim or combination)
- Food processor or flour mill (when leaf/trim is used)
- Clean or unused coffee grinder
- Flour sifter (optional)
- Frying pan or small saucepan
- Candy thermometer (optional)
- Gelatin capsules
- Capsule-filling machine
- Tamping tool (machine may come with one; otherwise, the head of a nail works well)

124

Ed:

Is there a way to make marijuana pills or capsules? I reek after smoking and I don't like to cook the stuff. When I consume marijuana I have a deeper high. Another reason why I want to consume rather than smoke it is to give my lungs a well-needed rest. Do you have any recipes or ideas?
Budd,
Internet

Budd:

My late friend Tom Flowers used to use Maricaps for his severe arthritis. He bought size O capsules and a filler holder that holds them upright. He used high-grade trim that was well dried and powdered fine in a coffee grinder. The powder was mixed with a few lecithin granules and enough olive oil to make a thick paste. Then the caps were filled and kept in the refrigerator or freezer until used.

Each cap held about a third of a gram of high-quality trim. Tom used them for relief of arthritic pain. Three or four caps on an empty stomach were quite potent. The advantage of caps is that you don't have to eat to use them.

The lecithin is added to help emulsify the THC. It's quite possible that a glass of milk (soy is okay), laden with emulsifiers, might help with the high.

Processing Leaf & Bud for Capsules

If the general instructions from trash collection in chapter one were followed, the leaf material should already have the stems and woody parts removed. Because the material used in capsules is reduced to a finer consistency than most processes call for, it is advisable to check the material for any smaller stems that remain. These too should be removed.

The material should be very dry before beginning this process. Place the material in the microwave for a minute or two, or spread the material on a cookie sheet and place it in an oven at 200 degrees F for 15 minutes to remove the last remnants of moisture.

Once the pot is stem-free and thoroughly dry, it is reduced to a fine powder. When it is being ground, the agitation causes the material to form clouds of dust. This "dust" contains many glands and should be retained if possible. It is best to be patient and let the dust settle before opening any containers.

A coffee grinder reduces the material to a sufficient powder for capsules. When starting with very coarse material, a food processor or flour mill can be used first. If the material contained a lot of leaf, the diligent processor can also follow the coffee grinding step with an additional sift using a flour sifter. This last step makes the material finer and more consistent. It also helps clean out any large or unwanted pieces that remain.

It is always better to have more powder than you plan to use, so if too much oil is added accidentally, a little more powder can also be added to reach the right consistency. Extra capsule powder is stored in the freezer. The refrigerator is also adequate. Cold, dark and oxygen-free conditions preserve marijuana's potency and protect it against molds or bacteria.

Making the Filling

Capsule machines may make 24, 50 or 100 capsules at a time. Since 0 capsules hold 0.3 grams and 00 capsules hold 0.6 grams, the amount it takes to fill 50 capsules is 15 grams (about 1/2 ounce) for 0 size and 30 grams (about 1 ounce) of 00 size.

Place the desired amount of material in a small frying pan or saucepan. Add a few tablespoons of oil, stirring to coat the material thoroughly. Place the pan over very low heat, 200 degrees F or lower. When warmed, the oil becomes thinner, which helps the material and oil to mix more readily. Keep the heat low to prevent scorching the material.

The oil-to-powder ratio may vary because leaf and bud absorb oil in different quantities. It will probably range between 3-6 tablespoons for an ounce of pot. Add just enough oil to make the material stick together in a dry paste-like consistency. Too much oil may not ruin the mixture, but will make filling the capsules more difficult. More powder should be added if the mixture becomes too oily.

The material only takes a few minutes to warm and mix thoroughly. After it has been evenly heated, remove from the stovetop. The mixture should keep the same dark green color. If the material turns brown, it has burned, which is bad. This material has lost most of its value. You should start over rather than continuing with this material.

To avoid the disappointment of burnt material, a more exacting method can be used. Heat the oil first, using a candy thermometer to monitor the exact temperature. Once the temperature reaches 200 degrees F, remove the pan from the stove and add the plant material to reach the proper consistency. The mixture can be encapsulated when it has cooled to room temperature (below 90 degrees F).

Filling the Capsules

Capsule machines have a platform with holes. The bottom of the capsule shells fit into this platform, and

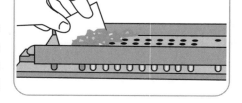

the oil mixture is pushed over it. The mixture must be tamped down into the capsules, repeating the process until they are completely filled. Sterilize a nail with the right-sized head, and use it for a tamper.

STORAGE

Optimally, maripills should be kept in a sealed, dark glass bottle or jar. They have a life span of only a few weeks at room temperature. In the refrigerator, they will keep for months. They can also be stored long-term in a

CAPSULE-MAKING TIPS

- Gelatin caps are derived from animal products. Vegetarian capsules can be used, but some types dissolve when oil is used in the filling. When buying vegetarian capsules, ask the salesperson if they can be filled with an oil-based mixture first.

- It is a good idea to process a little extra powdered material. This will allow the material-to-oil ratio to be adjusted if too much oil is accidentally mixed in.

- When material is being prepared for the capsules, it is briefly heated on the stovetop, which is capable of reaching very high temperatures. Remember that cannabinoids have boiling points between 350-390 degrees F—keep the burner set at a low temperature to avoid ruining the plant material's psychoactive and therapeutic properties.

- Bud absorbs more oil than leaf material. The amount of oil needed may depend on the ratio of leaf to bud and the type of oil used.

- Marijuana varieties differ in potency and cannabinoid content. Different strains may exhibit different highs and medicinal qualities. Likewise, using different ratios of trim, bud, leaf or kief will affect potency. Dosage should be reassessed each time a new combination of plant material is used.

frost-free freezer. However, due to condensation, they may stick together when brought to room temperature.

VARIATIONS

Tom Flowers recommended using alternate oils, such as hemp or flax, for additional anti-inflammatory effects.

Kief can easily replace the powdered leaf or bud. Especially for those who find plant material hard to digest, kief offers a cleaner alternative. When replacing plant material with kief, warm the oil first, and then remove from heat and add the material. It will not have a dark green color when mixed and heated because it does not contain plant matter. Also, keep in mind that the resulting pill will be more potent. The 0 capsules are recommended when using kief because they allow for smaller doses.

DOSAGE

Dosage will vary from person to person and from batch to batch, but it usually ranges between one to five 0 capsules or one to two 00 capsules.

If pills were made using only powdered bud, they will be more potent than a bud/leaf or leaf/trim mixture. Likewise, kief, which is a concentrated form of marijuana, will have higher potency and the dosage should be lowered accordingly.

Using different varieties of marijuana may alter the effects as well as the potency. Some varieties have higher contents of various cannabinoids, such as CBD or CBN, which produce their own effects. A strain with high levels of CBD, for instance, may have a more sedative or relaxing

effect, while a variety with more CBN may feel more strongly psychoactive or even disorienting.

Maripills can be taken at any time, but just like marijuana foods, results will depend in part on whether they are eaten on an empty or full stomach. When taken on an empty stomach, the onset of effects is more rapid, and the high may be more intense. Eating food right after the pills are taken may mitigate the potency and delivery. If maripills are taken after a meal, the effects will come on more slowly and the high may be milder.

RESOURCES

Gelatin Capsules,
Vegetable Capsules
& Capsule-Filling Machines:

Herbs 'n More.com
12574 Bennington Pl.
St. Louis, MO 63146
314-275-4955
501-423-1116 fax
www.herbsnmore.com

Herb Cupboard
P.O. Box 552
Elk Grove, CA, 95759
herb@herbcupboard.com
www.herbcupboard.com

Botanical.com
www.botanical.com
Herbal capsules in tools and accessories section

8

COOKING

E A T I N G cannabis foods is a healthy way to use marijuana without inhaling. It has a history that dates back centuries before prohibition. In 19th-century Paris, the Club de Hachichins met for the express purpose of eating hashish. Authors and poets whose works we now consider to be classics were members. In the 1920s, Alice B. Toklas published her infamous brownie recipe that popularized brownies as the cannabis food of choice in modern times. More recently, cannabinated foods have become a common therapeutic alternative for medical marijuana use.

Eating marijuana is a different experience than inhaling it. It is not an immediate rush. Instead, the sensation begins gradually a half-hour to an hour and a half after ingestion. The length of the lag time depends on a few factors. The high comes in "waves," reaching a peak an hour to an hour and a half after the first effects were felt. Then

it begins to taper to normal over the next hour and a half. Altogether, the high usually lasts three to four hours.

Taking the right dose is more important when ingesting than inhaling. Since the onset of the high is rapid when marijuana is inhaled, it is easy to self-titrate, that is, to find the proper level of high or medication. However, since the effects take longer to occur, it is harder to adjust the dose.

If you are unfamiliar with the effects, it is best to err on the side of too little than too much. You can always eat more, but you have to wait out the effects if they are too intense. This can be an unpleasant experience, but it is not dangerous. Your body will continue to function, and you will come down in a few hours.

Whether eating marijuana-enhanced foods as a regular method of ingestion, or just on special occasions, this chapter shows you how to transform your trash into four-star cannabis consumables.

The secret to creating tasty and effective cannabis food lies in transforming the cannabis into a cooking ingredient. This chapter focuses on the preparation of the basic building blocks that can be used in recipes of all kinds. A few simple recipes are included.

Using cannabis preparations and a little ingenuity, you will be able to turn tried-and-true favorites and cookbook recipes into cannabis treats. Recipes designed specifically for marijuana-enhancement are available in cannabis cookbooks and on the web. See the end of the chapter for recipe resources. If you aren't a consummate cook, you can always take the easy way out and use a ready-made mix. It is easy to make a good consumable once you understand how the THC is extracted and how the body processes eaten marijuana.

HOW IT WORKS
Food-Cannabis Chemistry

The first time I got high from ingesting marijuana, my host heated bottled tomato sauce. Then he added two teaspoons of ground trim that had been mixed into a tablespoon of olive oil. We were high by the time we stopped eating, and were stoned within the hour. I came down hours later.

It's obvious that cooking with marijuana is not rocket science; still, following a few simple procedures in preparing the herb will result in a better product and a more enjoyable experience. THC and the cannabinoids are not water soluble. In order to create a satisfactory cannabis consumable, the THC-bearing plant material must be combined with an ingredient that can dissolve it. Ingredients with this capacity are alcohol, oil, butter or fat-containing milk products.

Mild heat also has a role in cannabis cooking. Some THC on the marijuana plant is in the form of THC-A or THC acid. THC-A is THC with a carbonate molecule attached, and is much less psychoactive than THC. The attached carbonate molecule is COOH, (carbon, oxygen, oxygen, hydrogen). THC-A is easily converted to THC by detaching this COOH molecule using mild heat. This is called decarboxylation. When heated, the COOH molecule's tenuous connection to THC is broken, and it evaporates into the air as water vapor and carbon dioxide, leaving behind good ole' mindbending THC.

The heat must be mild rather than intense. THC has a boiling temperature of 392 degrees F. Once it reaches or passes this temperature, it begins evaporating into the air. To activate the THC without evaporating it, you must pay attention to the cooking temperature used.

In recipes such as the ever-famous brownies, the oven temperature is set at 350 degrees or higher. This is okay. The oven temperature climbs to 350 degrees or more but the batter never reaches this temperature. If you've ever had the joy of making a Thanksgiving turkey, you know that the oven is set at a temperature around 350 degrees, but the thermometer inserted into the bird only has to hit a temperature just under 200 degrees to be "done"—and a turkey cooks for hours. Baking temperatures indicate oven temperatures, not the temperature of the food.

The real danger of cannabinoid depletion is stove-top cooking. Sautéing or frying temperatures reach 400 degrees, above THC's boilng point, when cooking on high. The cannabinoids will boil off. Burning marijuana in a sauté can be the ruination of the entire venture. Stove-top cooking must be closely monitored to avoid cooking away the THC. The best way to use marijuana in a sauté is to add it when the dish is almost done. The active ingredient does not get a chance to heat up and evaporate.

When is Cannabis Edible?

If you've ever eaten raw buds or other plant material, you know that it can give you a buzz, but it is neither a very efficient, nor an appetizing method of consumption. Eating raw marijuana vegetative material is not like eating lettuce or celery—it is the human equivalent of a pet eating lawn grass. It isn't dangerous, but eating enough of it may leave you feeling green in a way you hadn't intended. Marijuana is closer to an herb than a vegetable when used in cooking. It can be added directly to foods such as soups or stews. The problem with using marijuana this way is that the taste may be objectionable to some people. If the pieces are too big, people may also find the texture unusual.

Ed:
I like to eat marijuana-laced food, but I don't like the taste of it. Is there any way to avoid getting that funky green flavor?
Lauren,
Nova Scotia

Lauren:
The solution is to eliminate the pigments and chlorophyll that gives marijuana-laced food its "green" taste. There are several ways to do this.

The first is to use kief rather than marijuana. Kief is a concentrate that already has the leaf material removed. It has little marijuana taste.

A second possibility is to clean the butter or oil before it is used in cooking. The pigments, such as chlorophyll, are water soluble so they can be separated from the butter by melting the marijuana butter, adding water and letting it simmer for a few minutes, then cooling it and throwing the water away. The process doesn't eliminate all the pigments, but it does reduce their presence.

Eating hash or kief is different than eating raw vegetation. Kief consists of the THC-containing glands, which are a fine golden to green powder depending on quality. Hash is the result when kief is pressed under warm conditions. The gland heads break and the oils emerge, forming a dense, sticky mass. Hash eating has a long history, both as a food additive and people swallowing pieces that slowly dissolve as they pass through the digestive system. Kief has only recently been available in the U.S., so it has not been used as much for ingestion.

The first time I ingested kief, it was mixed with olive oil and stuffed into an 00 capsule. The capsules were kept refrigerated until they were used. A single capsule was

enough for the evening. At times that evening, I thought I was living in slow motion.

Kief and hash have been eaten alone, but are better as additives in food. They are especially good as direct additives in a dish that already contains some oil, but since they are concentrated forms, much less is added, and it is important to make sure it is distributed evenly throughout the dish being prepared to avoid uneven results and problems with establishing a dose. Eating kief or hash can be taxing on the digestive system when eaten without processing.

Assimilation and Dosage:
What to Know Before You Start

Some people say that eating cannabis produces a more psychedelic experience than other methods of ingestion. The dosage, onset and experience of the high are all going to be different than anything you are accustomed to from smoking. Caution and companionship are both important ingredients for an enjoyable marijuana food experience.

Because of the chemical qualities of THC, assimilability changes depending on what is used to absorb and activate it. The method of processing the cannabis affects the length and intensity of the high.

Alcohol is the most rapid form of delivery, but is also the shortest lasting. THC dissolved in oil passes through the digestive system less efficiently than when it is dissolved in alcohol. Onset takes longer, too. However, THC is delivered to the bloodstream over a longer period of time so the high lasts longer. Some people think that butter takes even longer than alcohol to get into the bloodstream. While butter is the slowest form of delivery, it has the longest lasting effects.

Milk products absorb THC and other cannabinoids due to their dairy fat content. Because they are a combination

136

of water and oils, milk and soy milk also contain lecithin. Lecithin is a common emulsifier used in foods to break oil into small bits, which stay suspended in the water. The presence of lecithin in milk keeps it from separating. This is the same reason that commercial salad dressings stay mixed rather than separating into their oil and water constituents. The presence of lecithin speeds the absorption of milk products. They absorb faster than other oil or butter bases, but slower than alcohol.

When cannabis is eaten, it must pass through the digestive system before reaching the bloodstream. This takes time: an average of thirty to ninety minutes. The time varies from person to person, based on use pattern and weight, as well as how full the person is. The high from eating cannabis lasts between three and six hours, although overeating can extend the high for hours longer.

Marijuana's toxicity level is so low that it remains undetermined. Statistics suggest that a person would have to ingest several thousand times the typical amount of cannabis to reach a level that interferes with bodily functioning. To put this into perspective, coffee has fatal effects at 100 times the typical amount. Hence the truism that there are no casualties as a result of marijuana overdose.

It is possible to take a bigger dose than necessary to get the effect you were after. Eating marijuana can be one of the easiest ways to get too high. The delayed effect makes dosage harder to gauge and can lead to eating more than necessary. There is also an absence of the plateau effect. When smoking marijuana, a person often reaches a certain high and then stays about that high without getting noticeably more so, even if he or she continues to smoke. This plateau does not seem to happen when cannabis is eaten.

Ingesting too much cannabis is relatively harmless, but that does not mean it's pleasant. Try to avoid this problem in the first place by showing caution and restraint in eating cannabinated foods until a good dosage is determined. After all, it is always possible to eat more, but once it's in your stomach, there's no going back.

Treating Overdose

For those who do inadvertently find themselves in such a situation—and don't like it—there are a few things that can be done. The most important thing is for the person to realize that they are in no physical danger, even though they are experiencing a distorted reality.

In good company, an unpleasant experience may be eased by the comfort of others. The person should be encouraged to sit or lie down and try to relax, as dizziness may be one of the symptoms. Chills may be another symptom that is easy to treat by keeping the person warm.

Though the person will be high for 4 or 5 hours, the most intense feelings occur within an hour after the effects begin. Keep the person calm until then, and continue to reassure them throughout the 'peak' of the high.

Most of the time when a person has eaten too much, they will be excited and a little hyper for an hour or so, and then they'll tire and fall into a deep sleep.

Exerting caution when eating cannabis foods is a good idea, even for veteran smokers. Portioned sizes should be modest, and the amount of loaded food a person consumes, especially a guest, should be monitored. Needless to say, never give people spiked food without their knowledge.

Don't underestimate the temptation of the munchies. Prepare for them by having something else to snack on. This is especially a good idea when making a dessert dish

or something for a group gathering. Everyone can continue to snack without going overboard.

PREPARING THE HERB

Chapter 1 provides general guidelines for collecting and preparing trash for use. Following these instructions, all large stems should have been removed. If small stems are present, they must snap when bent, meaning they are dry.

Fresh material may be used when added directly to food, but dry material is called for when making butter or oil for recipes. Refrigerated or frozen cannabis retains its potency indefinitely and cold temperature stops microbial growth. If the plant material was stored wet, check for mold or bacterial attack. You can tell if pot is moldy by the mold visibly growing on it. Moldy pot is not suitable for

DOSAGE GUIDELINES

From *Marijuana Herbal Cookbook* by Tom Flowers

For a person weighing 150 pounds who has some experience using marijuana, a single dose is in the following range:

Marijuana Leaf:	**$1/2$ to 2 grams**
Average Bud:	**$1/4$ to 1 gram**
Sinsemilla:	**$1/8$ to $1/2$ gram**
Kief and Hashish:	**$1/8$ to 2 grams***

Using these guidelines, $1/4$ ounce makes the following number of servings:

Marijuana Leaf: 4-15 servings	**Sinsemilla:** 8-34 servings
Average Bud: 8-25 servings	**Kief and Hashish:** 4-34 servings

*Since kief and hash vary so much in potency, smoking some before using it in cooking will help gauge its strength. It's a tough job, but someone has to do it.

any use because it may contain toxins. Anaerobic bacteria are detected from the smell of ammonia that they release.

When making cannabis butter or flour, dried trim, leaf and bud bits are used, usually in combination. Regardless of how the trim and leaf was stored, it should be crispy and dry beforehand. To eliminate any residual moisture, microwave the material for a few minutes, or spread it on a cookie sheet and place it in a 200 degree oven for 10-15 minutes. An electric food dehydrator set on low can also remove any remaining water. Once the material is crispy, it's ready to use.

The glands are all on the surface area of the leaves, so they do not have to be ground to make contact with the oil or alcohol. Leaving the leaf material whole makes filtering it out much easier. Many cooks think that more cannabinoids are captured if the grass is crushed to the size of small herb flakes. This may be desired if the plant material is being left in the recipe.

Most cooks filter the marijuana from the recipe once the THC is extracted. However, some leave the ground pot in. To prepare pot for eating in this way, all the stems, even small ones, are removed. Then the material is ground to a fine consistency. A Cuisinart or blender quickly powders the material. Don't open the appliances immediately after use. Wait a couple of minutes for the gland dust to settle. Another option is to rub the dry material against a mesh wire strainer held over a container.

Using Hash, Kief or Hash Oil in Food

While this chapter focuses on using leaf and trim material to make ingredients, hash and kief are also good for cooking. They have a concentration of the cannabinoids without the vegetation, resulting in a cleaner, less "green" taste. Because they are concentrated, much less is

needed for each portion, but the cook must be careful that these ingredients are thoroughly mixed in to avoid uneven results. Hash oil may have been processed using petroleum ether or another organic solvent. Luckily, these solvents have low boiling points and evaporate quickly when exposed to the heat of cooking. Still, some people may not wish to use hash oil in cooking because of the solvents involved, and hash oil should not be used if the recipe does not call for any significant heating.

Hash, kief and hash oil need some preparation before they are used in cooking. Hash is shaved or chopped to a fine consistency. A coffee grinder, mini-chopper or a blender are all excellent tools for this purpose. Then the hash, kief or oil should be added to either cooking oil or alcohol and agitated. This is easily accomplished by putting everything in a small jar with a tight cover and shaking it, or by using a blender.

COOKING POINTERS

- Cooking with marijuana, especially leaf, can create some dank odors. Choose a place to cook where this won't be a problem.
- When deciding what to make, remember that snack foods or beverages make the best cannabis treats. Heavy foods like pastas are taxing on the digestive system—they will slow the onset of effects and may inhibit the amount of THC absorbed.
- Make sure the cannabis or cannabis ingredient is spread evenly throughout the dish for a consistent dosage.
- Remember the munchies? Some sources say they are even more pronounced when cannabis is eaten, so have some non-cannabis snacks on hand. Satisfy the munchie cravings without being tempted to overdo it on cannabis treats.
- Cannabis butters, oils or foods should always be marked to avoid accidental eating.

EXTRACT COOKIES

From *Marijuana Herbal Cookbook* by Tom Flowers

Mix together:
- 1/4 to 1/2 cup marijuana alcohol tincture
- 3/4 c softened butter
- 3/4 c sugar
- 1/2 c wheat germ

Sift in:
- 1 t baking soda
- 2 c flour

Beat until thoroughly mixed. Use a tablespoon to spoon onto an oiled cookie sheet. Bake at 300 degrees F for 20-30 minutes.

Yield: 25 cookies

Using Tinctures in Food

Tinctures can be a great addition to foods. They can replace ingredients such as vanilla extract in baked goods. Since tinctures are ready to consume, they can also be added to salad dressings or beverages, or at the end of food preparations. Tincture's alcohol base may give a rapid delivery when added to baked foods, while butter may pick up where the tincture leaves off and produce a long-lasting high. Keep in mind that adding tincture will increase the potency.

Honey elixir, which has alcohol and sugar in the base, is also great. See chapter 6 on tinctures to make your own extract or honey elixir. These can be used alone or with cannabinated butter to produce interesting and potent baked goods.

TRASH INTO TREATS

Just as no two cooks make the sauce exactly alike, there are many recipes, methods and techniques of preparing herb

for ingestion. The most popular ones are adding the herb directly to the recipe, dissolving the cannabinoids in butter, oil or alcohol, or using milk to dissolve and emulsify them.

Although people have tried adding cannabis to everything from soups and salads to meatloaves and lasagnas to desserts, some foods are better for delivery than others. Foods that contain the key ingredients in which cannabinoids dissolve will make the most efficient use of the THC in the plant material. Snack or bite-sized foods are better than heavy or filling dishes because they do not require the work a full meal demands of the digestive system.

ADDING DIRECTLY TO FOOD

I was dining at a grower's home. He said to me, "Notice the third shaker on the table?" There were three shakers: salt, pepper and golden glands—kief. "I use the glands on food all the time," he told me. "At first the grittiness got to me, but now I hardly notice it. It has sort of a nutty taste. When I add it to soups or saucy stuff, it melts after a few minutes and blends in. The glands tend to stick together in the shaker, so I added about 10 grains of uncooked rice. Problem solved."

Marijuana and kief can be added directly to food, just as you would another spice or herb. In fact, in Cambodia low-grade marijuana is for sale in the vegetable market for exactly that purpose. It is added to a dish just like parsley. Either whole sprigs or chopped pieces are used. This works best when the food to which it is added contains some oils or milkfats and undergoes mild or brief heating.

Finely ground trim or fan leaves can be used in soups, stews, sauces and gravies including curries, molés and barbecue sauce. The most important consideration when

BLAZED GUACAMOLE

From *Marijuana Herbal Cookbook* by Tom Flowers

Avocados contain 15% or more oil, making them a good food to mix with marijuana.

Mash together:

2 avocados	2 T sour cream
1-4 t ground marijuana leaf	1 clove minced garlic
OR	dash salt and Tabasco
1/2-2 g powdered sinsemilla flowers	

Refrigerate covered for 2 hours or more. Serve with corn chips and salsa. Variation: to make with cannabinated oil, omit the leaf or flowers and the sour cream, replacing with 1-4 teaspoons oil. **Yield: 4 servings**

adding magic spice to your recipe is to figure the number of servings people are likely to eat and to add enough, but not too much. People vary in appetite and tolerance, so it is best to err on the low side, rather than making the food too intense. Some people find raw kief, raw hash or uncooked plant material difficult to digest. These folks may have a more enjoyable gastronomic experience with cannabinated foods where the cannabis ingredient has been cooked in or the plant material has been strained out.

Some foods have too delicate a taste to absorb the complexity that cannabis lends to food. Many of the pigments and other flavorings can be removed from the cannabis before it is used. Soak the cannabis in room-temperature water for about 15 minutes before using it in the recipe. Strain the leaf from the water. Some of the green flavor and pigment will stay behind in the water, but the leaf will still hold the glands. They are ready to use in recipes.

Marijuana Flour

Ground marijuana is sometimes used as a direct replacement for part of the flour in a recipe, such as bread. I tasted one version made with whole wheat and other bread flours, including some hemp seed flour and finely ground marijuana flour. It had a pleasant, savory taste. When used as a replacement for flour, dried marijuana should only be used in a ratio 1 part ground leaf material to 2 parts regular flour to maintain a good texture and taste.

To turn leaf into flour, grind it in a clean coffee grinder. If the plant material is not in small enough pieces to use a coffee grinder, a food processor or flour mill can be used first. After grinding, a final sift using a flour sifter yields a marijuana flour with a consistency much like wheat bread flour.

Marijuana buttered flour is a more sophisticated flour replacement. Buttered flour has the benefits of potentiating the THC acid, dissolving some of the THC into the butter, and easing the digestion. It can also be used to replace the flour and part of the oil or butter in a recipe. Reduce the flour and butter based on the volume of buttered leaf added.

To Make Butter/Flour Mix:

Melt a cube (2 cups) of butter, margarine or oil in a skillet. Grind leaf in a blender or grinder to a flour-like substance. Add 1-1/2 to 2 cups leaf flour to the melted butter. Cook covered on lowest heat for 20 minutes. Stir to prevent burning, which would render the mixture useless. Add this flour to your standard recipe, reducing the flour and butter by the amount replaced with marijuana buttered flour.

MYSTIC MUFFINS

Adapted from *Marijuana Herbal Cookbook* by Tom Flowers
This basic muffin recipe has many possibilities to explore.

³/₄ cup marijuana
  buttered flour
¹/₂ c orange juice
1 c milk

¹/₂ c sugar
2-¹/₂ c flour
1 T baking powder

Melt buttered flour if not already melted, and place in a mixing bowl. Add orange juice, milk, and sugar and stir. Sift flour and baking powder together, and add to buttered flour mixture.

Add one of the following combinations:

- ¹/₂ c fresh or frozen blue-berries or raspberries
- ¹/₂ c almonds, pecans or walnuts
- ¹/₂ c chocolate chips

- 1-2 bananas mashed with 1 t lemon juice, ¹/₄ t nutmeg and ¹/₄ t cinnamon
- 1 t almond extract and 1-¹/₂ T poppy seeds

Stir just until ingredients are blended, then spoon into an oiled muffin tin and bake at 300 degrees for 20 minutes.   **Yield: 12 muffins**

GOT MILK?

Cow's milk is a complex of oils, proteins, sugars, hormones and enzymes. Regular milk contains about 3.5% butterfat, reduced fat milk contains 2% butterfat, and lowfat milk contains 1% butterfat. Since the cannabinoids dissolve in oils and fats, it is best to use regular milk to make cannabinated milk recipes.

All types of cow's milk and many milk alternatives, such as soy and rice milks, also contain the very powerful emulsifier, lecithin. The presence of both oils, which dissolve the cannabinoids, and an emulsifier, which holds

146

the cannabinoid-rich oil in suspension, makes milk an excellent food for ingesting cannabis.

"Homogenized" milk has undergone a process that breaks the fats into small particles from larger globules. This keeps them in suspension in the water base with the help of lecithin. Soy milk and rice milk also contain lecithin and about 1% fat. Coconut milk has a high fat content. These alternative non-dairy milks can be used in place of cow's milk in most marijuana-milk recipes. If a non-fat milk or milk substitute is used, some fat should be added to create a soluble medium. Simply mixing in a tablespoon of plain oil or butter will enhance the milk's extraction properties.

WAMM'S MOTHER'S MILK
From Wo/men's Alliance for Medical Marijuana: www.wamm.org

1 oz. leaf that has been crumbled to a flour consistency
2 qts. whole fat milk (soy, cow, goat, coconut etc.)

Combine leaf and milk in crockpot and cook on low for a minimum of 2 hours. WAMM recommends a cooking time of 8 to 12 hours. Do not open. Do not stir. Do not worry. The medicine might float, that is fine. Strain the leaf from the mixture using a cheesecloth- or pantyhose-lined strainer. (For more thorough instructions on straining, see butter straining instructions p. 159.) That's it.

Spices, such as cinnamon, nutmeg, or ginger, can be added near the end of the cooking process or after milk is finished for an eggnog-type flavored milk. Vanilla or chocolate can also be stirred in when getting ready to drink.

Depending on potency, serving sizes may range from 1/8 to 1/4 cup.

Drink WAMM Mother's Milk fresh by itself or in other beverages. It can also be frozen. Measure 1/8 cup servings and fill an ice-cube tray. They can be removed and melted or defrosted in the microwave to enjoy when desired.

For marijuana milk that can be enjoyed as is or combined with other beverages, follow the suggested recipe for WAMM's Mother's Milk. WAMM stands for the Wo/mens Alliance for Medical Marijuana. In the fall of 2002, the federal government raided this exemplary self-help, non-profit medical marijuana cooperative based in Santa Cruz, California.

CannaTea, Lassies & Chai

When cannabis is brewed with milk it makes an effective tea. Some teas are brewed with a slice of butter. The fat content also helps increase the tea's potency.

To make tea, heat milk until it simmers. Add apportioned leaf or trim and keep at a simmer for 15-30 minutes. Strain the milk and pour into a teapot containing the appropriate number of bags or tea leaves. Allow the tea to steep for 5-10 minutes. Drink and enjoy.

In India, where milk and milk products are dietary staples, bhang balls are used in some entrees. They are also used to make bhang lassies. I first experienced bhang while traveling through India. It was available everywhere

BHANG LASSI

From *Marijuana Herbal Cookbook* by Tom Flowers

1 c milk	$1/2$ t cardamom
1-2 t ground leaf flour OR	1 t rose water
$1/2$-1 gram powdered	dash cinnamon, nutmeg
sinsemilla flowers	or clove
2-3 T sugar	2 c yogurt

On low heat, mix together all ingredients EXCEPT yogurt. Heat to near boiling. Simmer 30 minutes or more. Cool and strain. Mix in yogurt. Drink cold. **Yield: 2 servings**

I went. The preparation of a truly traditional bhang lassi is somewhat elaborate, requiring the repeated grinding of spices into a paste with mortar and pestle. The quick, simplified version given on the previous page is also quite delicious.

Indian chai is a black tea brewed with spices including clove, cinnamon, cardamom and ginger. It may also include vanilla beans, black pepper or anise as well as Indian spices not generally available in the U.S. (commercial chai mixes are available). The tea is mixed with equal parts of water and hot milk. The milk and spice combination make a soothing drink with an unusual and enjoyable taste. Chai is especially suitable for taking a head trip. Exotic spices gently transport you from your everyday to a soothing tranquility. Soon the first waves of highness float into your mind. Exquisite.

Water-based CannaTea

Cannabinoids are not water soluble, so making a tea by boiling buds, leaf or trim in water will not extract them. Many of the pigments and terpenes that give marijuana its color and flavor are water soluble, so the water may take on a color and aroma that seem promising. However, these elements of the plant do not contain the psychoactive cannabinoids. The wet, boiled plant material still contains cannabinoids and can be used for additional extraction processes.

It is possible to prepare a weak tea by boiling plant materials because the heat and agitation will cause a portion of the THC to separate from the leaf material. The separated cannabinoids will float loose in the water, but they won't dissolve into the water the way sugar dissolves. When ingested, it may have a weak psychoactive effect.

A tea made from plant materials and water is not the most effective way to ingest cannabis, nor is it the most efficient way to get all the THC from the plant material, but it can have an enjoyable, mild effect. Heated milk can be added to the tea to increase its potency and taste. Marijuana teas are common folk medicines used for upset stomachs of children and adults in Jamaica.

CannaCoffee Drinks

Coffee's rich complex flavors make an enjoyable marijuana beverage. In some regions of the world, hashish and coffee are considered a classic combination. The mixture of THC and caffeine may hasten the onset of the high. Caffeine also increases marijuana's stimulating properties and can counterbalance lethargic or sleepy effects.

There are several ways to make cannacoffee beverages. If coffee with milk is desired, WAMM's Mother's Milk (p. 147) can be used to make a knockout café au lait. Hash can also be used. It is first measured for dosage and crumbled or finely shaved. Then it is added to a small amount of warmed milk over the lowest heat and stirred until it has dissolved and become thoroughly blended. The warmed milk is added to prepared coffee.

To enjoy a cannacoffee beverage that doesn't contain milk, consider adding tincture or honey elixir to prepared coffee. Hash can also be added directly to coffee. It should be finely ground. Combine the hash with already made coffee in a small pan over low heat. Stir for a few minutes until the hash has thoroughly dissolved and is mixed evenly in the drink.

Some people add chocolate powder to create a dessert-like drink. Turkish coffee often uses a pinch of powdered cardamom with hash for an aromatic and spicy coffee

drink. Once the warm ingredients are blended, the resulting beverage can be sweetened and served warm or over ice.

CANNABINATED COOKING OIL

All cooking oils dissolve cannabinoids and easily transport them through the digestive system to the bloodstream. Once oil is cannabinated it can be used for salad dressing and in many recipes. However, using it in high temperature sautés or in frying food raises the temperature above 392 degrees F, the boiling point of THC and the other cannabinoids, so they boil away.

It is easy to make cannabinated oil. One method is to simply add leaf, trim, bud or kief to cooking oil. I first saw this in a friend's kitchen. Just as you can make oils with chili peppers or tarragon, my friend decided to infuse a quart of virgin olive oil with one ounce of bud. He added the pot, and then sealed the bottle and let it sit

PSYCHEDELIC SALAD DRESSING

From *Marijuana Herbal Cookbook* by Tom Flowers

Combine in a jar:

1/4 c olive oil	3 T balsamic vinegar
1 small clove minced garlic	2 T water
1-3 t marijuana leaf flour	2 t soy sauce
or 1-2 grams powdered	1 t sugar
sinsemilla flowers	pepper to taste
2 T wine	1/2 t lecithin

Combine and shake up all ingredients. For best results, let sit for an hour or two. Pour over a large salad. Use bread to sop up excess dressing.

Yield: 4 servings

151

for a month before he began using it for a very wild oil-and-vinegar dressing.

There are ways of quickening the cannabination process. The non-water methods described for butter in the next section can also be used for oil. The double boiler or crockpot methods are recommended. Similar ratios apply with oil as with butter (see p. 153). This translates to 1 cup of oil to 1 ounce of plant material. Since less oil is sometimes used for recipes, stronger oil may be desired. For particularly potent oil, the amount of plant material can be doubled.

Measure your oil and plant material and add to the top pan of the double boiler or crockpot. If using a double boiler, add water to the bottom pan. Heat the mixture over a low simmering heat for 1-4 hours, stirring occasionally. Strain or don't, as desired. Pour back into the bottle. A funnel might be useful.

The potency of cannabinized cooking oil stays strong for a long time if sealed and stored in a cool, dark place. Storing in the refrigerator is a good idea.

Cannabinized cooking oil can be used in recipes that list cooking oil as an ingredient. Sauces and salad dressings are ideal because the temperature never rises above water's boiling point, far below THC's boiling point.

CANNABUTTER FOUR WAYS

Cannabutter is a favored method for cannabinating foods, especially those of the sweet variety. It is possible to make as little as half a stick of butter or as much as multiple pounds. Recommended cooking times vary and are open to experimentation and adjustment. Times can be shortened for smaller amounts, but shouldn't exceed the longest times suggested.

Potency: Butter and Plant Material Ratios

When butter is used in a recipe, the cook must take into account the potency of the butter and the amount of butter in the dish to come up with an appropriate serving size.

Some chefs prepare all of their butter at the same ratio and adjust the serving size based on how much butter is in the recipe. For this method, the recommended ratio is one ounce dried cannabis material per one cup of butter.

Using this method, cookies in a recipe that calls for one cup of butter and makes 20 cookies would be more potent than a recipe that makes 20 cookies but only contains 1/2 cup of butter. Serving sizes adjust according to the recipe.

If the amount of butter called for in a recipe will make the desired serving size (for example, one cookie) too potent, then only substitute cannabutter for part of the regular butter. Figuring ratios by this method is best when butter is being made in bulk all at once, and then used as needed.

Other cooks make the butter according to the serving size. The ratio is approximately one gram per serving. For instance, if a recipe for cookies calls for a 1/2 cup of butter and makes 8 cookies, then 8 grams, or about a quarter ounce, of the dried trim, leaf and bud bits are prepared in the 1/2 cup of butter. If another recipe made 16 servings, but still only contained a 1/2 cup of butter, then twice the amount plant material would be used to make the butter. This method of figuring serving size may be better if butter is made to be immediately used.

Making cannabutter is an inexact science, since the potency of the trim and leaf used may vary from batch to batch. These methods and ratios offer a good baseline approximation that can be adjusted as needed depending on what is known about the material being used. Regardless of the method used, the serving size will have

to be considered when starting a recipe: Do you want to get high off of a teaspoon of butter spread on toast? Do you want to be able to eat a WHOLE cookie without going overboard? Adjust ratios to suit these preferences.

The Methods

One source for making great butter and oil comes from the company "Tainted," a baked goods and cannabis chocolate supplier to medicinal clubs in California. Pioneered by Guy, who has been cooking for a living for 15 years, Tainted has worked on perfecting the butter-making process to get a good tasting and potent product. He offers two methods for home cooking: the double boiler method and the crockpot method.

Double-Boiler Method

EQUIPMENT AND INGREDIENTS

- A stovetop
- Double boiler, or 2 pots that can be used like a double boiler
- Cooking mitts
- Dry plant material
- Butter
- Metal strainer and/or new pair of nylon panty hose
- Water
- Stirring utensil

A double boiler is essentially a two-pot system, where one pot fits inside another (see illustration). The diameter of the inside pan is about an inch smaller than the outer pan. The sides are high enough on the inside pan so that no water gets into the ingredients. It is sufficient to use two pots that fit together in approximately the same fashion. The large pot is filled with water and placed directly on the burner. The smaller pot holds the ingredients and is placed inside the large pot.

Measure the butter and dry marijuana leaf, and place together in the smaller pan. Add enough water to the bottom pan so that when the ingredient pan is placed inside, the water comes to a level above the ingredient mixture. Put the bottom pan on at a medium heat and place the ingredient pan in it. Stir as the butter melts to saturate the marijuana mixture.

Once the bottom pan reaches a boil, lower the temperature to a simmer or a low setting on your stovetop. The butter/marijuana mixture will stay at 212 degrees F or less, the boiling point of water, as long as there is water in the bottom pan. Cover the top pan with a lid and check back often.

Guy recommends cooking for a minimum of 8 hours and a maximum of 14 hours. Stir regularly. The water level in the bottom of the double boiler will also need to be monitored. Add water to the bottom pan to keep the level higher than the ingredients in the top pot.

Guy believes that before the minimum 8 hours, the butter has not absorbed as much THC as possible. More than 14 hours and the butter tastes burned. At about 12-14 hours, Guy starts getting the color he wants—the butter turns a dark green.

When finished cooking, lift the small inner pot from the outer one and set it on a potholder. The cannabutter must be strained. See instructions on straining p. 159.

Don't put the double boiler away yet! Use it to make some chocolatey treats.

KILLER FUDGE

From *Marijuana Herbal Cookbook* by Tom Flowers

Melt and mix on low heat or in a double boiler:

1/4-1/2 c marijuana butter

10 oz. bittersweet or milk
  chocolate

1 c sugar

1/2 c half & half or milk

1/4 c cocoa

1/4 c chopped walnuts
  or pecans

Spread on a shallow baking pan and cool, then cut.

Yield: 14 squares

Crockpot Method

Double boiling is a very good method, and is especially recommended when cooking in quantity. However, if the batch is to be small, and you are looking for less hassles, the best bet might be the crockpot method. Crockpots are inexpensive and are specifically designed to simmer foods at low temperatures for long periods of time.

EQUIPMENT AND INGREDIENTS

- Crockpot
- Dry plant material
- Butter
- Stirring utensil
- Metal strainer and/or new pair of nylon panty hose

Measure the butter and plant material, and place in the crockpot. Temperature control is easy because the crockpot is designed for low simmering. Set the temperature on low, at approximately 200 degrees F. Cover and let cook, stirring at regular intervals. Guy's cooking time recommendation remains a minimum of 8 hours and a maximum of 14. See instructions on straining, p.159.

To Use Water in the Crockpot Method:

- Add 2 cups of water for each cup of butter in the crockpot.
- Follow directions given for crockpot method above.
- Allow about half of the water to boil off, but add water as necessary to keep some water content present in the mixture through the end of the process. Cook as directed above. At the end of this time, refer to straining instructions when using water, p. 161.

WHY SOME BUTTER METHODS USE WATER

Many cannabis butter recipes recommend adding water to the butter and trim when cooking. There are three main reasons that water is used in butter recipes:

1) **Less "green" flavor**. Cannabinoids are not water soluble. Water does not absorb any of the THC or other cannabinoids, but it does wash out some of the chlorophyll, which gives cannabis butter its green color and "green" taste. The popular vote on this issue is mixed. Some people prefer the green color and taste. Others would rather mask or minimize it. Keeping the green taste has one advantage: it is a clear indication that the goodie is "enhanced." To safeguard against any surprises, cannabinated foods should always be labeled.

2) **Better temperature control.** As mentioned in the beginning, stovetop temperatures can easily soar above 392 degrees F, burning the butter and boiling off the THC, leaving only a bum product. The presence of water keeps the temperature from rising above 212 degrees F. Crockpots and double boilers are other ways that the temperature is maintained.

3) **Water allows more plant material to be mixed in.** While the dosages given are plenty good using the average trim, it is important to have enough liquid content so the marijuana is not just absorbing all the butter and burning the plant material in the pan.

Methods that work with water are the Stovetop Water Method and the Crockpot Method.

The Stovetop Water Method

Miss Jesse, the first cook I saw make cannabutter, had a great recipe. She decided to make her butter so that one tablespoon would be a serving size. The problem was that there was not enough liquid for the extraction. The leaf absorbed most of the butter. Her solution was to add 2 cups of water to each cup of butter. She boiled the mixture for about half an hour. The water absorbed the pigments and flavors while the fatty part of the butter absorbed the cannabinoids. She strained out the plant material, then cooled the mixture in the refrigerator and pulled the butter from the top of the pot. She threw the water away.

EQUIPMENT AND INGREDIENTS

- A stovetop
- A big sauté pan or frying pan
- Cooking mitts
- Dry plant material

- Butter
- Metal strainer or new pair of panty hose
- Water
- Stirring utensil

Instead of keeping the water and butter separated in a double boiler setup, water and butter are combined in one pan, and are separated at the end of the process.

For each cup of butter being used, bring 2 cups of water to a rolling boil. (So if you are making 2 cups of butter,

use 4 cups of water.) Add the butter and plant material. Lower the heat to keep a moderate boil. Add more water by the cup as the water level lowers. Cook for 30 minutes to 3 hours, checking the heat level and water content. Stir regularly.

At the end of this time, strain out the plant material as directed in the straining section below.

Stovetop Method

So long as it is carefully monitored and not allowed to burn, the stovetop method can be a quick and easy alternative to long simmering butter-making processes.

EQUIPMENT AND INGREDIENTS

- A stovetop
- A big sauté pan or frying pan
- Cooking mitts
- Dry plant material
- Butter
- Metal strainer or new pair of panty hose
- Stirring utensil

Measure the butter and plant material and place in a large sauté or frying pan. To extract as much THC as possible without losing it to evaporation, gently simmer the butter over low heat. The water content in the butter boils at about 212 degrees F, well below the 392 degree F boiling point of cannabinoids. Some cooks let the mixture simmer for a whole day, but virtually all the cannabinoids dissolve in fifteen minutes. See straining instructions below.

STRAINING THE BUTTER

Once the butter mixture has finished cooking, it must be strained before the process is complete.

There are a few typical straining methods. Some people simply use a fine wire-mesh strainer, although plant material will escape into the final product using this method. Cheesecloth or pantyhose, as directed below, can be used as a liner within the strainer for finer results.

Panty Hose Straining

Guy prefers to use a new pair of panty hose to strain out the plant material. He swears it is the best thing—easier to use than pastry cloth or cheesecloth, less likely to rip or break, easier to squeeze out and more efficient since less butter is absorbed into the straining material itself.

The material can be poured into a leg of clean pantyhose held over a clean container. A large funnel may be helpful to this process. The nylons can also be secured to a regular metal mesh strainer and sieved into a bowl. Once all the trash rests in the pantyhose, it can be lifted and wrung out. Wait for the mixture to cool, since hot fats can cause wicked burns.

Putting the Squeeze On

While the pantyhose method will offer the best results with the least chance of ripping, the material should be squeezed carefully but thoroughly to recover the most butter. The butter that is soaked into the leaf material will be quite potent and is worth a little extra effort. If a mesh strainer was used, it is possible to squeeze the material over the strainer with gloved hands. Pastry cloth or cheesecloth should be carefully pressed to recover material. Twisting the cloth tightly may result in rips that allow plant material through.

Some butter will remain in the material even after it is pressed tightly. To remove the remaining, potent butter

GREENIES

From *Marijuana Herbal Cookbook* by Tom Flowers

Cookies are a great choice for cannabination. This basic, easy recipe is ready in under an hour. Greenies are not too sweet and are very palatable.

1) Mix together:
- 1/2 c melted cannabutter
- 3/4 c milk, soy milk, or half & half
- 1/3 c flour
- 1 egg

2) Beat for 5 minutes. Add in:
- 3/4 c sugar
- 1 t orange extract (optional)
- 1/2 t nutmeg (optional)

3) Sift in:
- 1 t baking powder
- 2 c flour

Beat with a mixer until thoroughly blended. Spoon onto a greased cookie sheet by the tablespoon. Bake at 300 degrees F for 25-30 minutes.

Yield: 28 small cookies: a serving size is one cookie

from the grass, suspend it over a new clean bowl, and slowly pour boiling water through the grass into another container. The butter will melt and drain out with the hot water. Once this water/butter mixture is allowed to cool, the butter will rise to the top and harden. It can be separated from the water once it has cooled and hardened, and the water can be tossed out. This process is hastened by placing the mixture in the refrigerator.

Straining with a Water Method

When water is cooked with the butter, the method is essentially the same. The plant material is separated from the butter and water using one of the methods described. A second strain with hot water is still beneficial. It need only be poured through into a separate bowl if the first one has become too full.

The strained liquid will be a combination of water and butter. Put the mixture in the refrigerator until the butter solidifies. Once the butter is solid, separate it from the water.

REFILTER FOR FLAVOR
If a butter recipe has been prepared using a non-water method and is found to be particularly harsh-tasting, it is not too late to get the advantages of water. Heat the butter and add twice as much water as there is butter. Allow to heat to a low boil and cook for 15-30 minutes. The water will still remove some of the harsh flavors and probably some of the color from the butter. Once it cools, the butter can be separated from the water.

CHANGING THE INGREDIENTS

Using Hash or Kief instead of Marijuana

It is really easy to make hash and kief into butter. They are simply measured to a desired potency and blended with melted butter. It is not necessary to cook the mixture for long periods, since the cannabinoids have already been separated from the plant material. The material is heated over low heat in a pan with the butter until the hash has dissolved. Since hash and kief are more concentrated, care must be taken to ensure that the hash or kief has been evenly distributed throughout the butter. No water or straining is necessary since there isn't any extraneous plant material. Once the kief or hash dissolves and is well-mixed into the melted butter, it is ready to use.

Using Margarine instead of Butter

Butter is the oil of choice among bakers, although some chefs use margarine. Margarine, like butter, is a combination of fatty oils and water. Both butter and margarine

contain lecithin, which helps oils mix with water in suspensions. Most brands of margarine contain more water than butter does. The water boils off during cooking, leaving less final product. Figure that for every pound (2 cups) of margarine you start with, the end result will be about 3/4 lb (1-1/2 cups).

Clarified Butter & Ghee

Clarifying the butter removes the milk solids and water from the butterfat. When butter is placed under medium heat it melts and then begins to foam. If the heat is turned to low the butter continues cooking. First the foam disappears. Then the butter begins to crackle as the water boils off. The milk solids fall out of the oil, sinking to the bottom of the pan. The butter turns a deep clear yellow, as only the oil is left. The oil is lactose free. The result is clarified butter.

The process is essentially the same for ghee as for clarified butter. The difference is that, with ghee, the milkfat is allowed to brown slightly, giving the final product a flavor that is alternately described as "caramel," "butterscotch" or "nutty." Ghee has a long shelf life and can cook at even higher temperatures than regular clarified butter.

Ghee is the pure oil of the butter. It has a very buttery taste and forms a soft solid at room temperature. A pound of butter will result in about 3/4 of a pound of ghee. Ghee can be cooked at a higher temperature without burning. It is also free of impurities.

You don't have to make ghee in order to use it. Ghee is available at Indian markets and some other grocery stores. Clarified butter and ghee make excellent cannabinated oils. However, leaf should be processed in a double boiler or crockpot to assure that the temperature remains low enough so the cannabinoids don't evaporate or boil away.

QUICK & EASY BUZZ FOODS
Once prepared, cannabutter is ready to eat. Try it spread on a slice of bread or your morning croissant or muffin.

Yogurt is a really easy and healthy way to enjoy cannabis. You can add cannabis oil or tincture to ready-made yogurt for a quick lift. For a more potent snack, mix in kief or hash to make some wacky yogurt.

Tinctures can be added to cold or warm drinks for a refreshing and relaxing beverage. Try stirring into a glass of lemonade, cranberry juice, or adding to tea just before drinking.

FOOD ADVENTURES

If you want to explore the world of cannabinated food beyond brownies, here is a list of food suggestions:

- Flavor extracts, particularly orange extract, seem to neutralize cannabis odors. Just add a teaspoon to any cookie or cake recipe. Orange extract imparts a nice fruity flavor to baked goods and is good with chocolate. Orange extract can also be used when making marijuana butter or oil.

- Strong spices such as ginger, cinnamon, cloves or nutmeg mask the smell of marijuana when making baked goods. A teaspoon in cookie recipes blends well with the taste of marijuana leaf. Chocolate also helps neutralize the smell of marijuana, and disguises any green coloration.

- Light foods and snacks are the best match when looking for recipes to cannabinate. Some yummy foods we recommend as candidates for cannabization:

  - Hummus
  - Dips
  - Pesto
  - Banana bread and other dessert breads
  - Chocolate pudding
  - Ginger cookies, peanut butter cookies or your other favorite cookie recipes

STORAGE

Cannabinated foods are the same as other marijuana products. Heat, light and oxygen deplete THC over time. When eggs, milk, butter or other perishable ingredients have been used in a recipe, it should be stored in the refrigerator, or for longer shelf life, in the freezer. Sealed, opaque containers protect the THC from exposure to oxygen and light.

RECIPE RESOURCES

Books:

Marijuana Herbal Cookbook, by Tom Flowers

Brownie Mary's Marijuana Cookbook and Dennis Peron's Recipe for Social Change, by Mary Rathbun

Stir Crazy, by Quick American Archives

Gourmet Cannabis Cookery: The High Art of Marijuana Cuisine, by Dan D. Lyon

The New Marijuana Cookbook: Recipes for Recreation and Health, by Tom Flowers

Web Sites:

www.letfreedomgrow.com
www.fyuocuk.com/ potcooking01.html

www.greencookbook.com/
www.disabilityuk.com/cannabis/ cannabiscooking_recipies.htm

Topical Uses of Marijuana

Plant material can be saved and used topically to provide relief for localized pains. Scientifically, cannabinoids are categorized as "lipophilic." This means that they are absorbed into the cell membrane, so they can be applied topically with some effect. Marijuana poultices have been mentioned as folk remedies in several cultures.

When applied topically, the cannabinoids are not usually absorbed in large enough quantities to get you high. Most people report that topical applications have no psychoactive effects. A mild buzz is most likely if it is applied in liberal quantities. Using marijuana oil on the entire body may even make a person too high. It is better to experiment with lower amounts first to gauge the effects. This will differ from person to person based on tolerance level.

Anecdotal evidence suggests that marijuana is effective for various topical uses. In order to work, the material must still retain some cannabinoid content. Material that has already been processed has little medicinal value. New scientific evidence continues to emerge on the cannabinoids' effects on the body. Current research is studying marijuana's effectiveness for the treatment of inflammation and migraines. Other reported uses for marijuana balms and oils include muscle soreness, rheumatism and eczema or psoriasis.

As with the many processes described in the book, the active constituents in marijuana absorb more readily and evenly when they have been processed in a soluble medium. THC and other cannabinoids are soluble in alcohol and fats, including oils.

Cooking oils made with marijuana (chapter 8) can be used topically, especially when made with oils friendly to the skin, such as olive oil. If the oil is being made solely for topical use, try using light almond oil, or coconut oil. Cocoa butter can also be prepared for topical use following a butter preparation method (chapter 8).

Balms can be made from already prepared cannabis oil using beeswax or aloe vera.

CannaBee Topical Balm:
Melt 1/3 cup beeswax and mix together with 1 cup of cannabis oil. Allow the mixture to cool, and store in a sealed container in a cool, dark place. Other medicinal oils can be substituted for a portion of the cannabis oil to make a multi-medicinal balm.

CannaLotion:
Thoroughly blend 1/2 cup cannabis oil with 1 cup aloe vera gel. Store in an opaque sealable container. Aloe vera is good for sunburns and sensitive skin. It stores well in the refrigerator.

Tinctures can also be used topically. When used for specific local pain, a highly concentrated tincture is best. Once the tincture is made following the directions in chapter 6, there are no adjustments for topical use. Obviously, if topical use is intended, it is better to prepare the tincture with a non-colored and non-flavored alcohol. Food-grade glycerin is sticky and does not make a good topical application. Alcohol, especially if an overproof type was used, may sting or dry the skin. Anecdotally, tinctures are suggested for relief from arthritis, muscle pain and spasms.

Finally, plant material that still contains some cannabinoids can be saved and used directly. Some people may freeze plant material that has been processed for water hash or tinctures. To use this material as a poultice, it is thawed, wrapped in cheesecloth and applied to the injured or sore area. Plant material that has already been processed has a weaker cannabinoid content and its effectiveness is minimized as a result. People claim to use this as a folk remedy for sore muscles or local aches and pains.

The Cannabinoids

At present, 483 distinct and identifiable natural chemical components are known to exist in the cannabis plant. Many of these, such as amino acids, sugars, hydrocarbons and proteins, are ubiquitous throughout the plant and animal kingdom. But 66 of these—known as the cannabinoids—are found in marijuana and nowhere else in the natural world.

The cannabinoids present in the greatest quantity are THC, CBN, CBD and CBC. Each of these types has several subclasses. For instance, there are five CBC-type cannabinoids and seven CBD-type cannabinoids that differ in appearance and effect because of slightly different side-chain molecular structures. THC also has several sub-classes with varying levels of psychoactivity.

Delta-9 THC (delta-9 tetrahydrocannabinol) is marijuana's main psychoactive ingredient. It accounts for most of the high. THC is also primarily responsible for appetite stimulation. Actually, THC is found in nine variations with slight differences in their chemical structure. Four or five of these variants have similar effects to THC. For instance, THC-V (tetrahydrocannabivarin) is a variant of THC found in some varieties of Asian and African grass that seems to be much faster in onset and quicker to dissipate than standard THC. Even though THC-V's psychoactivity appears to be somewhat less than that of THC, it is usually associated with extremely potent grass.

All THC appears in fresh plant material with a COOH molecule attached. In this form, THC is called THC-A or THC acid, and is only weakly psychoactive. The use of heat—in smoking or processing plant material—removes the COOH molecules, a process called decarboxylation. Removing the COOH molecule, renders an active form of THC.

THC occurs in all varieties of cannabis, in concentrations that vary from trace amounts to about 95 percent of all the cannabinoids present.

CBN (cannabinol) is produced by the degradation of THC. It is very weakly psychoactive, at

best about 10% of THC's effect. Fresh samples of marijuana contain very little CBN, but curing, poor storage or processing can cause the THC content to be oxidized into CBN. When grass is pressed for shipping, the resin glands that hold and protect THC are sometimes ruptured, exposing the cannabinoids to air and increasing the rate of oxidation.

CBN seems to potentiate THC's disorienting qualities, making one feel more drugged, dizzy or generally untogether, but not necessarily higher. With a significant proportion of CBN, the high may start well and then feel as if it never reaches its peak, and may not last long.

CBD (cannabidiol) also occurs in almost all cannabis varieties in quantities that range from trace amounts to 95 percent of all the cannabinoids present. In its pure form it is not psychoactive, but it does have sedative, analgesic and antibiotic properties. CBD contributes to the high by interacting with THC to potentiate or antagonize certain qualities.

CBD appears to heighten the depressant effects and to moderate the euphoric effects.

It may also delay the onset of the high, but makes it last considerably longer. Terms such as "knockout," "sleepy," "dreamlike" and "contemplative" are often used to describe the high from grass with sizeable proportions of CBD. In 2001, GW Pharmaceuticals found that only a combination of CBD and THC offered analgesic effects for Multiple Sclerosis patients. Taken alone, neither CBD nor THC was as effective in treating chronic pain as they were in combination. CBD may also be effective in reducing intraocular pressure, the medical application for glaucoma patients.

CBC (cannabichromine) is inactive in its pure form, but is suspected of potentiating THC. Some tests made for CBD may actually have measured CBC, which is chemically similar.

CBG (cannabigerol) is a non-psychoactive cannabinoid. Studies suggest that it may reduce intraocular pressure and contribute to marijuana's antibiotic properties.

Equivalents and Conversions

Measurement Abbreviations

t	=	teaspoon
g	=	gram
T	=	Tablespoon
kg	=	kilogram
c	=	cup
mL	=	milliliter
pt.	=	pint
L	=	liter
qt.	=	quart
oz.	=	ounce
lb.	=	pound

Fluid Equivalents

3 t	=	1 T	=	15 mL
4 T	=	$^1/_4$ c	=	60 mL
1 c	=	8 oz.	=	240 mL
2 c	=	1 pt.	=	473 mL
2 pts.	=	1 qt.	=	0.94 L

Dry Equivalents

$^1/_4$ oz.	=	7 g		
$^1/_2$ oz.	=	14 g		
1 oz.	=	28.4g		
8 oz.	=	227 g		
16 oz.	=	454 g	=	1.lb.
1000 g	=	1 kg	=	2.2 lbs.
100 kg	=	a federal rap		

U.S. Food Measures

Butter:	1 lb.	=	2 cups
Flour:	1 lb.	=	4 cups
Sugar:	1 lb.	=	2 cups

Temprature Conversions

Fahrenheit	Celsius
150	66
212	100
250	120
275	135
300	149
325	163
350	177
375	191
400	204
425	220
450	230
475	240
500	260
550	288
600	316

Powdered Marijuana Leaf & Bud

1 t	=	1.8 g		
1 T	=	5.5 g	=	~$^1/_4$ oz.
$^1/_4$ c	=	22.4 g		
$^1/_3$ c	=	28 g	=	1 oz.
$^1/_2$ c	=	45 g		
$^2/_3$ c	=	56 g	=	2 oz.

Screen Sizes

100 microns = 0.1 millimeter = 0.0039 inches

75-125 micron screen = approximately 100-150 strands per inch screen

Typical marijuana gland size range: 75-125 microns

Terms

conduction: heat transfer through solid matter, such as metal. A conduction vaporizer has a metal or other hot element as its heat source.

convection: the transfer of heat by automatic circulation of a fluid. A convection vaporizer circulates hot air or fluid to produce the proper temperature.

decarboxylation: simply means the removal of a carboxyl. A carboxyl is a carbonate molecule (COOH). Carboxyl molecules are sometimes attached to the THC molecule which is then called THC-A, or THC acid. In this form, THC lacks most of its psychoactivity. Decarboxylation removes the COOH acid molecule, leaving behind THC. Mild heat is often used to convert THC-A to THC. This happens during drying, vaporization and smoking.

emulsifiers: promote suspension of small fatty globules in water. When water and oil are mixed together, they quickly separate. However, in the presence of an emulsifier the oil breaks into small bits suspended in the water. Two examples of this are milk and commercial salad dressings. Lecithin is a common emulsifier that is available in health food stores.

leaf: in the context of this book, the term is used to connote fan or large sun leaves, as well as the larger secondary leaves.

loupes: Used by photographers, a loupe is essentially a magnifying glass. It can be used to observe the plant surfaces. I find that an 8x loupe is sufficient for this purpose. Inexpensive 30x plastic scopes can apparently be found in toy stores.

mixtures: A mixture is a suspension of a non-soluble compound in water. Milk and gravy are examples.

oxidation: the action of oxygen when it unites with another substance chemically. This happens quickly in fire, but also takes place on a much slower level at room temperature. For marijuana and its products, oxidation is deterioration. The oxygen content of air interacts with marijuana to reduce the THC content.

poultice: a mollifying remedy of a moist nature applied to inflamed surfaces. Poultices often contain minerals, herbs or other medicinals.

pyrolytic compounds: compounds produced by chemical change brought about by the action of heat. These compounds often consist of carcinogenic hydrocarbons.

self-titrate: this is to determine a dosage for oneself.

sinsemilla: the name given to the seedless buds harvested from an unfertilized female marijuana plant. Because the flowers were not pollinated, the plant puts more energy into producing flowers, which increases the yield. Sinsemilla is often used to generically refer to potent marijuana.

solution: when a substance dissolves, its molecules actually form a loose molecular relationship with the liquid that it dissolves into; for instance, sugar in hot water or chlorine in a pool are solutions. Their molecules spread out so that they are evenly spaced throughout the liquid.

sublingual: a method of using tinctures. The liquid is placed and held under the tongue and is absorbed by the porous mucous membranes lining that part of the mouth. When consumed in this way, absorption is faster than eating because it does not have to pass through the digestive system, but is slower than smoking. This is a good way to use marijuana for the treatment of nausea without inhaling.

titration: dosage.

trichomes: a three- or four-celled gland with a bulbous head that stretches as it fills with THC and other cannabinoids.

trim: consists of the small leaves that surround and protect the buds. Aside from the buds themselves, the trim has the most concentrated cannabinoid content.

References

In addition to reports from vaporizer reviewers and interviews with vaporizer inventors, tincture makers, cannabis chefs, water hash bag manufacturers, kiefers, hash pressers and other cannabis-creative folks, the following books, articles and web sites served as sources for this book. Entries are listed in alphabetical order by title.

The Art and Science of Cooking with Cannabis, by Adam Gottlieb. CA: Ronin Publishing, 1993.

"A brief survey of hash making techniques," by SCW. *Cannabis.com Magazine,* 2002. http://www.cannabis.com/ezine/accessorize/2.shtml [August 2002].

Cannabis and Cannabinoids: Pharmacology, Toxicology, and Therapeutic Potential, by Franjo Grotenhermen, MD and Ethan Russo, MD editors. NY: Hayworth Integrative Healing Press, 2002.

Cannabis for Lunch, by Eric. UK: self-published, 2000.

Cooking with Cannabis, by Tom Hodlin. E-book: http://www.fyuocuk.com/potcooking.html [September 2002].

Cooking with Ganja, by Eric. Self-published in the UK: 1997.

Cooking with Marijuana, by Evelyn Schmevelyn. WA: Sun Magic Publishing, 1974.

Hashish by Robert Connell Clarke CA: Red Eye Press, 1998.

"Hash with Oldtimer1," by Oldtimer1. *Overgrow Magazine,* 2002. http://www.overgrow.com/iss1/m_hashwithot_1.html [Sept. 2002].

"How to Judge Hashish," by ZeroZero. R*ecreational Drugs Information,* 2002. http://www.a1b2c3.com/drugs/hash011.htm [Oct. 2002].

"How to Make Wicked Hash," by Liza Scammell and Bianca Sind. *Cannabis Culture* 36 (April/May 2002): 88-92.

Marijuana Growing Tips, by Ed Rosenthal. CA: Quick American Archives, 1999.

Marijuana Herbal Cookbook, by Tom Flowers. CA: Flowers Publishing, 1995.

"Marijuana in capsule form," by Martin Martinez. *CannabisMD*.com, 2002. http://www.cannabismd.com/reports/mjcapsules.php [Oct. 2002].

"Marijuana Water Pipe and Vaporizer Study," by Dale Gieringer. *Multidisciplinary Association for Psychedelic Studies (MAPS) Newsletter*: vol. 6, no. 3 (Summer 1996).

The Science of Marijuana, by Leslie L. Iversen. Oxford University Press, 2000.

"Smokeless Marijuana," by August Salemi. *Online Pot: The Complete Guide to Medical Marijuana*, 2002. http://www.geocities.com/onlinepot/smokelesspot.htm [Oct. 2002].

Stir Crazy: Cooking with Cannabis, by Quick American Archives. CA: Bobcat Press, 1999.

"The Superior Vaporization Technique," by the Real Real McCoy. CA: VripTech Int., 1998.

"Tincture," by Jay R. Cavanaugh. *American Alliance for Medical Cannabis*, April 2002. http://www.letfreedomgrow.com/recipes/tincture.htm [July 2002].

A Treasury of Hashish, by Dr. Alexander Sumach. Toronto: Stoneworks Publishing Company, 1976.

"Vaporization of Cannabinoids: a Preferable Drug Delivery Route," by Tod H. Mikuriya, M.D. *Shaffer Library of Drug Policy*. http://www.drug library.org/schaffer/hemp/vaporize.htm [Aug. 2002].

"Vaporizers for Medical Marijuana," by Bruce Mirken. *Aids Treatment News* 327 (Sept. 17, 1999). http://www.aids.org/immunet/atn.nsf/page/a-327-02 [Sept. 2002] or http://www.aegis.com/pubs/atn/1999/ATN32702.html [Sept. 2002].

"Vaporizing Cannabinoids: Inhaling Safely," by Tod H. Mikuriya, M. D. *Mikuriya.com*, 2002. http://www.mikuriya.com/vaporize.html [Oct. 2002].

Plus various web site articles from:
www.cannabis.com
www.kief.com
www.letfreedomgrow.com
www.overgrow.com
www.ukcia.org

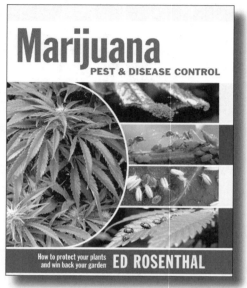